At the age of nineteen, **Kenny M** with 'social anxiety disorder' and ev carry on working. As the years passed, he became almost housebound as a result of his illness and as such lost touch with many parts of life which, although enjoyable, are often taken for granted. Simple pleasures such as buying a nice sandwich from a local café or going out for a meal became impossible for him to do.

As a result of this, and because of his love of food and cooking, he eventually took to trying to recreate many of his favourite shop-bought foods at home. 'If I can't go to McDonalds, I'll make my own,' was his philosophy. Over a period of five years or more he tested and tweaked many, many recipes, his new hobby quickly building into an obsession.

In 2010, Kenny decided to publish some selected recipes in his first book *The Takeaway Secret*. It became an instant bestseller, following word-of-mouth recommendations on the Internet.

With huge support and encouragement from readers, his confidence has grown, along with his food obsession. As a result, Kenny once more ventured out into the world, researching and learning about the historic links between street food and local people and the recent upsurge in the modern, exciting and vibrant street food culture. His next book, *The Street Food Secret*, was released in 2017, quickly followed by *The American Diner Secret* in 2019 and *The Indian Takeaway Secret* in 2021. Kenny's passion for recreating delicious takeaway/restaurant and street food-style dishes remains as strong as ever!

ALSO BY KENNY McGOVERN

The Takeaway Secret
More Takeaway Secrets
The Street Food Secret
The Takeaway Secret (2nd edition)
The American Diner Secret
The Indian Takeaway Secret

THE CHINESE TAKEAWAY SECRET

*How to Cook Your Favourite
Fakeaway Dishes at Home*

Kenny McGovern

ROBINSON

ROBINSON
First published in Great Britain in 2022 by Robinson

1 3 5 7 9 10 8 6 4 2

A CIP catalogue record for this book
is available from the British Library.

ISBN: 978-1-47214-691-5

Typeset in New Caledonia by Hewer Text UK Ltd, Edinburgh
Printed and bound in Great Britain by Clays Ltd, Elcograf S.p.A.

Papers used by Robinson are from well-managed forests and other responsible sources.

Robinson
An imprint of
Little, Brown Book Group
Carmelite House
50 Victoria Embankment
London EC4Y 0DZ

An Hachette UK Company
www.hachette.co.uk

www.littlebrown.co.uk

How To Books are published by Robinson, an imprint of Little, Brown Book
Group. We welcome proposals from authors who have first-hand experience
of their subjects. Please set out the aims of your book, its target market
and its suggested contents in an email to howto@littlebrown.co.uk.

NOTES ON THE RECIPES

Eggs used throughout the book are medium-sized eggs.

Any neutral-flavoured vegetable oil may be
used (I typically use sunflower oil).

To thicken stir-fry sauces and soups, a mix of potato starch and
water is indicated in recipes. Mix this well before use and add
when soups or sauces are at a medium rolling boil, stirring the
mix in thoroughly to ensure a thickened sauce without any
lumps. When cooking several dishes, ensure you have more
potato starch/water mix than you feel you need, in order to
ensure that you don't run out while dishes are simmering.

When purchasing spices, try not to buy more than you
need for the foreseeable future – fresh spices will add
great flavour to your dishes while older spices will have
lost some of their flavour and aroma over time.

Oven temperatures relate to conventional ovens – for
fan-assisted ovens, the cooking time should be reduced
slightly, or the cooking temperature lowered by 20°C.

Most of the recipes in this book can be scaled up or down
as desired, providing the quantity ratios remain consistent.
However, when cooking curry sauces, proper reduction of the
sauce is desired, so I suggest cooking one portion at a time.

CONTENTS

INTRODUCTION

Chinese takeaway food regularly comes top in studies of the UK's most beloved fast-food cuisines, and if you've experienced it, you'll know why. With flavours ranging from savoury to spicy, to sweet and sour and all that falls between, there's something for everyone on a Chinese takeaway or restaurant menu.

Despite being classed as fast food, UK takeaway chefs work tirelessly day and night in order to create the wide variety of dishes they offer. Preparing ingredients, marinating meats, cooking stocks and sauces all take time, so you can be sure that the staff in your local takeaway are hard at work long before opening time comes around. Luckily for you, whether as a customer in your local outlet or as a budding chef in your own kitchen, with prior preparation taken care of, it takes just minutes to dish up all manner of tasty treats.

As well as making classic dishes that have been known and loved for generations, such as curry, sweet and sour or satay, Chinese takeaways are ever-evolving and in recent years the rise in popularity of 'salt and chilli'-style dishes has been huge.

In order to keep up with the latest offerings and to pick up inspiration as well as a tasty meal, be sure to pay a regular visit to your local takeaway.

Suitably inspired and heading for the kitchen, you'll soon find that Chinese takeaway-style food is amongst the most fun to cook. With ingredients and a hot wok at the ready, delicious dishes can be produced in a matter of minutes. I hope the recipes in this book will help you to recreate some of your fast-food favourites.

EQUIPMENT

Carbon-steel wok – A good-quality carbon-steel wok is relatively inexpensive and will, if seasoned and cared for correctly, last a lifetime. These woks can sustain extremely high heat, offering the famous 'wok hei', or 'breath of the wok', to stir-fried dishes.

Deep-fat fryer – When deep-frying, ensuring your oil reaches and maintains the desired temperature results in food that's crispy and delicious without being greasy. To that end, a good deep-fat fryer can be useful. A wok or large saucepan filled a third full of oil will do the same job; however, it's worth investing in a temperature probe in order to monitor your oil's temperature. (See page 21 for advice on deep-frying.)

Non-stick wok – While a well-seasoned carbon-steel wok is suitable for high-temperature cooking and gives flavourful results, a good-quality non-stick wok is also useful for some dishes, particularly omelettes and foo yung dishes. If you're new to stir-frying, it's not a bad idea to use a non-stick wok until your confidence grows, at which point you may prefer to try a carbon-steel version.

Rice cooker – I cooked rice for over twenty years without using a rice cooker, having always been perfectly happy with the results I got from cooking in a saucepan on the hob. When I look back on it, I'm surprised that I didn't get one sooner, especially considering how many kitchen gadgets I'm so easily tempted to invest in. Having now purchased a rice cooker, I can say with confidence that it's an excellent addition to any kitchen (as if you needed me to tell you that – millions of Chinese, Thai, Malaysian and Vietnamese cooks aren't wrong!). As well as the added convenience of a timer and 'keep warm' settings, a good rice cooker produces perfect rice every time, with the bonus of leaving your hob space free for stir-fry dishes.

Steamer – Bamboo steamer sets are inexpensive and can be used in a wok for steaming siu mai (Chinese dumplings). The gentle heat results in deliciously soft dumplings.

Wok brush – A well-seasoned carbon-steel wok needs nothing more than hot water and a scrub with a wok brush after cooking.

Wok ladle – A ladle is ideal for stirring in the potato-starch-and-water mix to thicken soups and stir-fry sauces.

Wok stirrer – A flat 'shovel'-type stirrer is useful for tossing food in the wok.

HOW TO CHOOSE, SEASON AND
USE A CARBON-STEEL WOK

Non-stick woks and frying pans come in all shapes and sizes nowadays and I've certainly used a few of them over the years with good results. If you're serious about stir-frying, however, investing in a proper carbon-steel wok is a smart decision. If you've cooked with non-stick pans often, you'll know that over time the coating inevitably wears off, making cooking difficult and risking the possibility of some of that coating going into the food you intend to eat (which is far from ideal). A properly-seasoned wok creates a natural non-stick layer which ensures you can cook over a high heat with consistent results over time. Even more importantly, a carbon-steel wok can withstand high heat which can add great flavour to your meals.

Choosing a carbon-steel wok

Most carbon-steel woks are suitable for all hob types, but do check before buying. Woks come in various sizes, with either a round-bottom or flat-bottom finish. For home use, a flat bottom is the one to choose; round-bottom woks typically are intended for use over the gas burners in takeaway and restaurant kitchens. When it comes to choosing the size of your wok, it's best to go for something in the small to medium range. For one-portion cooking (which is ideally how you want to stir-fry anyway), a flat-bottomed 30cm carbon-steel wok is ideal. The wok heats quickly and holds its heat so well that each portion cooks in just a few minutes so it's easy to prepare 3–4 portions one after the other if need be. Of course, if you have a larger hob you can choose a larger wok to suit your own needs. Expect to pay £8–£10 for a good-quality carbon-steel wok from Chinese supermarkets, or a little more online. To accompany your wok, you might choose to purchase a wok stirrer for cooking and a wok brush for cleaning.

Seasoning your carbon-steel wok

When you've got your carbon-steel wok, you'll have to season it before you begin to cook with it. This essentially means burning off the manufacturer's coating, which is on the wok, cleaning the wok out and heating it with oil to form a natural non-stick layer. A good seasoning on your wok will give you a pan that you can use again and again. In fact, the performance of the wok should even improve over time with extended use.

Step 1:
Give the wok a good clean in hot soapy water, rinse and dry completely. This is the one and only time you'll use washing-up liquid on your wok – from this point on it should require nothing more than water, heat and a scrub with a wok brush.

With the carbon-steel wok washed and fully dried, open any nearby doors and / or windows and put the wok on the hob over a high heat. This is much easier to do on a gas-flame hob, but with time and patience it's possible to do it on a ceramic, electric or induction hob also. This process creates a lot of smoke and a noticeable aroma, it is unpleasant but an important part of seasoning your wok. As the wok gets hot, you'll see it begin to change colour and appear to blacken. Tilt the pan over the high heat until all the coating is removed and the surface of the pan has changed colour – this will take a few minutes. When the coating has burnt off completely, remove the wok from the heat and set aside to cool. Rinse the wok out with water and a wok brush, dry completely again and return the pan to the hob. Switch the heat on low for 5 minutes in order to help ensure the wok is completely dry before moving on to Step 2 of the seasoning process.

Step 2:
Slice a selection of stir-fry vegetables (onions, spring onions, garlic, ginger, peppers, etc.). Heat the wok over a medium heat until it just begins to smoke. Add 1 tablespoon vegetable oil and the prepared vegetables and stir-fry for 15–20 minutes, until the vegetables are almost burnt. The idea here is simply to spread the hot oil around the wok and the vegetables will be discarded, so feel free to use old/inexpensive stir-fry vegetables. Again, you'll notice the wok change in colour a little and appear well-used compared to the brand-new silver shiny wok you started with. After 15–20 minutes, empty out and discard the vegetables. Allow the wok to cool, rinse out again with water and scrub with a wok brush, dry with a clean tea towel and place over a low heat for 5 minutes to dry completely. Add a little oil to the wok and wipe it all around with kitchen

7

paper until the entire surface is coated. Switch the heat on to medium-low and allow the wok to sit over the heat for 10 minutes.

Your seasoned wok is now ready to use.

Using and caring for your carbon-steel wok

At this stage, with a high heat and some oil, your wok should have some good non-stick qualities. Over time, the natural patina will build on the wok and performance should improve with regular use.

Things to remember when cooking with your wok:

- Always heat the wok over a high heat until just smoking before adding oil. Cooking over a high heat will help to ensure that food doesn't stick.
- When adding marinated meat to the wok, allow the meat to settle in the pan for 10–15 seconds before stir-frying. Allowing the meat to settle in the pan will help to ensure it doesn't stick, which is particularly useful when the marinade includes cornflour or potato starch.
- Use a wok stirrer to scrape and stir the ingredients in the wok during cooking, ensuring the ingredients don't catch in the pan any more than desired.
- After the wok is fully preheated, add enough oil for the dish you plan to cook – restaurant chefs often add more oil than is necessary to the pan then drain off any excess, ensuring the entire surface of the wok is coated.

- In the early days of owning your wok, try to avoid cooking acidic dishes (dishes with vinegar, lime juice, etc.), boiling or steaming with the wok.
- Conversely, deep-frying with lots of oil in the wok will assist in building the natural non-stick patina.

To care for your wok, simply wash it out after each use with water and scrub it with a brush.

Things to remember when cleaning your wok:

- Allow the wok to cool before cleaning, in order to avoid shock from drastic temperature changes which may warp the shape of the pan.
- Use only hot water and a wok brush to clean your carbon-steel wok – washing-up liquid isn't necessary. If the wok needs more vigorous cleaning, add a little water to the wok and heat until boiling. This will ensure any ingredients in the wok simply slide away and it can be easily cleaned.
- Keep your wok clean and dry at all times – drying with just a tea towel isn't enough. Return the clean, dry wok to a low heat on the hob for 5 minutes in order to ensure it's completely dry.

Apply a little cooking oil around the entire surface of the wok with a piece of kitchen paper before storing the wok for future use.

By ensuring your carbon-steel wok is completely clean, dry and coated with a little oil after each use, it should remain rust-free with a natural non-stick coating and last a lifetime. Should rust appear in your wok, don't panic! Simply scrub off any noticeable spots with a wire brush, wash the wok out well with a brush and hot water and allow to dry completely. Repeat the seasoning process again and your wok will be returned to its former glory.

STORE-CUPBOARD
INGREDIENTS

When it comes to Chinese takeaway-style cooking, there are some essentials which will help you achieve the flavours you desire. Listed below are ingredients I like to keep well stocked. It's worth paying a visit to your local Chinese supermarket if you're lucky enough to have one in your area – one look at the products offered for sale in large amounts will quickly give you a clue as to which brands are used often in takeaway kitchens!

Bamboo Shoots – Used mainly for their texture, tinned bamboo shoots are a great vegetable addition to stir-fry dishes.

Beetroot Powder – While many takeaway restaurants continue to use artificial food colourings, I prefer to use beetroot powder to colour sauces. Just a small amount mixed with a little water adds a delicious deep red colour to Sweet & Sour Sauce (page 200) and Chinese-style BBQ Sauce (page 206).

Chicken Powder – Chicken stock powder can be found in Chinese supermarkets and is great for making chicken stocks or simply for adding flavour to marinades.

Chinese 5-spice – This aromatic spice mix includes fennel, star anise and cloves and is an essential ingredient in Salt and Pepper Seasoning (page 214). When shopping for Chinese 5-spice, look for brands that include orange peel in the ingredients list.

Chinese Ginger Powder – Also known as sand ginger, this adds great flavour to Salt and Pepper Seasoning (page 214).

Creamed Corn – This can be found in tins in Chinese supermarkets or online, and is used to make Chicken and Sweetcorn Soup (page 80).

Custard Powder (original, not instant) – Used to add a slightly sweet flavour and beautiful golden colour to crispy meat dishes.

Dried Black Fungus – This edible mushroom can be found in packets in Chinese supermarkets and has a long shelf life. Simply rehydrate in hot water before adding to Hot and Sour Soup (page 81) or your favourite stir-fry.

Dried Chilli Flakes – Used to add heat to the Szechuan-style Stir-fry (page 125) and salt and chilli dishes.

Fermented Black Beans – These salty fermented black soy beans have a long shelf-life so are well worth keeping in your cupboard. You'll find them in tubs or packets in Chinese supermarkets – they are a very different product from tinned black beans which are typically used in Mexican cuisine. Mix with garlic and stir-fry ingredients for the Black Bean and Green Pepper Stir-fry (page 121). A teaspoon of prepared fermented black beans can also be added to a Szechuan Stir-fry (page 125) with good results.

Fish Sauce – Primarily used in Thai dishes, a little fish sauce goes a long way and adds a delicious umami flavour to the mix for Sesame Prawn Toast (page 63).

Flour (plain, self-raising, potato starch) – I use plain flour for the crispy coating on my Chicken Wings (page 52) and use self-raising flour for the Chicken Balls (page 30), Salt and Chilli Pizza Crunch (page 100) and French-fried Onion Rings (page 189). Potato starch is used to thicken stir-fry sauces (page 99) or in the coating for crispy chicken or king prawns, etc. Cornflour is an acceptable substitute, but potato starch offers superior results.

Garlic Granules – These dried garlic pieces can be rehydrated, gently fried in oil and then stored in the fridge for use in stir-fry or salt and chilli dishes.

Golden Syrup – Use to sweeten stir-fry sauces or marinades.

Ground Fish – Pungent and flavourful, ground fried fish can be found in Chinese supermarkets and is used to top Crispy Seaweed (page 74).

Ground White Pepper – Earthy and mildly spicy, ground white pepper adds good flavour to soups and stir-fry sauces.

Hot Bean Sauce – This sauce adds a delicious spicy element to various dishes including Hot and Sour Soup (page 81) and Szechuan-style Stir-fry (page 125), as well as being a key flavour in Dan Dan Pork Noodles (page 144) Look for jars labelled 'hot bean' or 'doubanjiang' or 'toban djan' in Chinese supermarkets or online.

MSG (monosodium glutamate) – The ingredient which has suffered more undue criticism than any other. Despite widespread fearmongering from worried rival Western food producers, MSG has been proven to be perfectly safe, time and time again. Found naturally in ingredients such as broccoli, cheese, tomatoes and more, the seasoning labelled 'MSG' in food packets in Chinese supermarkets brings out the delicious umami flavour in stir-fry dishes and much more. If you haven't embraced it already, make a point of doing so!

Noodles (thick and thin) – Essential for chow mein and noodle soup dishes, you'll find huge boxes full of these in Chinese supermarkets. Lucky Boat noodles are made from wheat and are widely used in Chinese takeaway restaurants. Somewhat surprisingly, this widely used noodle brand doesn't contain egg, making it ideal for vegan chow mein dishes! Vermicelli noodles (rice noodles) are ideal for Singapore-style Chow Mein (page 171) and Yuk Sung (page 72).

O.K. Sauce – A savoury mix of tomatoes, tamarind, vinegar, fruits and spices, this sauce is full of flavour and can be found bottled in Chinese supermarkets.

Oyster Sauce – Thick, flavourful and savoury, this sauce forms the base of so many stir-fry sauces. Mushroom stir-fry sauce can be used as a vegan alternative.

Peanut Butter – Used to add delicious savoury flavour to Satay Sauce (page 129) and Dan Dan Pork Noodles (page 144). Smooth or crunchy both work well, so try experimenting with your favourite nut butters!

Rice – Jasmine and long grain (page 159).

Rice Wine – Just a splash of this aromatic wine gives a beautiful finish to stir-fry sauces or salt and chilli dishes; it also works well in marinades. Dry sherry works as an acceptable substitute if necessary.

Saté Sauce – The famous 'Jimmy's'-brand saté sauce provides the well-known satay sauce flavour that Chinese takeaway customers know and love.

Sesame Oil – This fragrant and aromatic oil can be added to soups and other dishes towards the end of cooking to add a final burst of flavour. Sesame oils vary greatly in strength of flavour, with pure oils offering a light and sweet finish to dishes in contrast with a stronger nuttier flavour from toasted sesame oils. With a little experimentation, you'll find one that best suits your tastes (I like Korean pure sesame oil!). Sesame oil (especially toasted sesame oil) should be used at the end of cooking to finish a dish and not as your main cooking oil. Light sesame oil can be used for frying at lower temperatures, but I prefer to cook with sunflower or vegetable oil and reserve sesame oil for finishing dishes.

Smoked Garlic Powder – Garlic powder dissolves well in sauces for added flavour. Since we don't typically have access to takeaway-style burners when home cooking, I like to use smoked garlic powder to add extra flavour; however, you can use regular garlic powder instead.

Soy Sauce (light and dark) – Used extensively in marinades and sauces throughout this book, light soy sauce is salty and used to season dishes whereas dark soy sauce is less salty, a little thicker and adds deep, rich colour. It's well worth visiting your local Chinese supermarket to source soy sauce – supermarket own-brand soy sauces are very diluted and won't offer the same results.

Sugar – Widely used to balance the flavour profile of stir-fry sauces, marinades and curries.

Tomato Ketchup – Adds a delicious tangy sweetness to char-siu marinades and can be used to good effect to add just a little sweetness to stir-fry sauces.

Vinegar – A variety of vinegars, including rice wine vinegar, distilled clear malt vinegar and Chinese black vinegar (chinkiang), are used to add acidity and tang to soups and sauces.

Water Chestnuts – Despite the name, water chestnuts aren't actually nuts, but are in fact an aquatic vegetable that grows underwater. Light and crunchy, they add good texture to stir-fry dishes.

FRESH INGREDIENTS

Baby Sweetcorn – Crunchy and slightly sweet, baby sweet-corn is a great addition to vegetable soups or stir-fry dishes.

Beansprouts – Fresh and crunchy, beansprouts are an important ingredient in chow mein dishes, or can be stir-fried as a side dish. You can grow your own in just a few days (page 221).

Carrots – Used mainly for colour, thinly sliced carrots can be poached briefly in water to soften them slightly before drain-ing and adding to your favourite stir-fry dish. Alternatively, cut into matchsticks and use in salt and chilli dishes.

Chillies – Fresh sliced chillies are often used as a spicy garnish for stir-fries and can be added to salt and chilli dishes.

Garlic – Fresh garlic can be used in stir-fries or salt and chilli dishes. It can burn easily though, so be sure to stir-fry it quickly when cooking. Alternatively, chopped garlic in oil (page 211) is a flavourful and very convenient alternative.

Ginger – Fresh ginger is used to make aromatic oil (page 212) or can be used in stir-fry dishes and soup stocks.

Mushrooms – Full of natural umami flavour, wok-fried mushrooms are spectacularly tasty and make a good addition to any stir-fry dish or soup.

Onions – The aroma and flavour of sliced onions cooked in a roaring-hot wok is enough to encourage any appetite. Try to purchase larger onions for longer slices that will form the basis of a huge variety of dishes.

Peppers – Crisp, colourful and fresh, the perfect vegetable addition to any stir-fry.

Spring Onions – Full of fresh flavour as well as adding colour to dishes, you'll definitely want to keep spring onions in stock if you're a fan of salt and chilli dishes!

ADVICE ON DEEP-FRYING

It's not uncommon for home cooks to be a little intimidated by deep-frying. While it does pay to be cautious, with some simple tips in mind we can easily and safely deep-fry at home, even without the aid of a deep-fat fryer. If you plan to deep-fry often and like to keep your hob spaces free, investing in a good-quality deep-fryer is worthwhile; however, any large wok or pan can be used to good effect – simply fill the pan a third full with sunflower oil or any neutral-flavoured cooking oil which can be heated to high temperatures for deep-frying (such as vegetable oil, rapeseed oil, peanut oil, groundnut oil).

If you use a wok or a pan for deep-frying, investing in a temperature probe is a must. These can be purchased relatively inexpensively and will ensure your oil reaches the desired temperature before frying, guaranteeing crisp and golden results without any excess grease.

Most deep-frying recipes call for oil to be heated to about 180°C/350°F; however, do check individual recipe instructions for precise temperatures.

Deep-frying tips:

- Use a temperature probe to ensure your oil has reached the desired temperature before carefully adding food items.
- Avoid overcrowding the pan as this lowers the temperature of the oil and can result in greasy food. Instead, fry in batches and keep each fried batch warm in a low oven, or re-fry cooked food briefly to reheat and crisp it up once more, just before serving.
- A slotted spoon / spider strainer is useful for removing cooked food from the oil while allowing excess oil to drain off.
- A fine-mesh strainer can be used to remove smaller food remnants from the oil. This will ensure that they don't burn and keeps the oil cleaner.
- After cooking, ensure the pan with the oil is set aside in a safe place until it has completely cooled down.
- Strained oil that is free from food remnants may be reused several times; however, you'll soon find that oil which has been used to fry breaded items such as Crispy Chicken (page 28) or Chicken Wings (page 52) becomes cloudy and discoloured more quickly. For this reason, I like to bulk-fry these items and often fry a double or even triple batch at one time.

PREPARING AND COOKING MEAT, FISH AND TOFU

Prior preparation prevents poor performance they say, and this certainly applies when it comes to cooking. When dishes are made up of various layers of flavour (and prepared entirely from scratch), it can be useful to divide the work into sections, particularly when some jobs can be done ahead of time. This chapter includes recipes for marinading and cooking chicken, pork, beef, king prawns and tofu for use in various dishes. In some instances, these items can even be prepared and cooked in bulk, cooled and stored in the fridge or freezer for future use when called upon. With a freezer stocked full of tasty precooked items, you'll be minutes away from combining them with your favourite sauces for a takeaway-style feast!

CHICKEN BREAST

Serves 1

Chinese takeaways often use chicken with added water and salt, which helps to ensure that the meat remains tender after cooking. You can find chicken like this in most supermarkets and in frozen-food stores.

This recipe uses fresh chicken with a simple marinade and brief poaching, to ensure the sliced chicken has a texture similar to that which you'll find in your favourite takeaway dishes. The method requires a small pan of boiling water to poach the meat briefly just before stir-frying. This extra step is well worth it for the results it delivers.

1 skinless, boneless chicken breast fillet (about 150g),
    thinly sliced
Pinch of sea salt
Pinch of MSG
Pinch of ground white pepper
1 tablespoon water
1 teaspoon vegetable oil
1 teaspoon potato starch

- Put the sliced chicken, sea salt, MSG, white pepper and water in a bowl, mix well and set aside for 5 minutes. Add the vegetable oil and mix well. Add the potato starch and mix well once more. Set aside for another 5 minutes.

- When you're ready to cook your stir-fry dish, fill a pan with water and bring it to the boil. Add the sliced chicken to the boiling water, bring back to the boil and simmer for 2 minutes until the chicken is sealed and just cooked through. Strain the chicken through a colander and it's ready to be added to your favourite stir-fry dish.

- Alternatively, let it cool completely and keep it in the fridge for up to 2 days, or freeze for up to 3 months. Reheat the sliced chicken thoroughly (defrosted if frozen) in a boiling stir-fry sauce for 2 minutes until heated through.

CHICKEN THIGHS

Makes enough for 2 main dishes or 6 soup dishes

This simple poaching method ensures deliciously tender chicken, which can be sliced and used in stir-fries, soups or chow mein dishes.

500ml Light Chicken Stock (page 218) or low-salt chicken stock from a cube
½ teaspoon sea salt
¼ teaspoon MSG
¼ teaspoon ground white pepper
450g boneless, skinless chicken thighs (about 5 thighs)

- Bring the chicken stock to the boil in a pan over a medium-high heat. Add the sea salt, MSG and white pepper and mix well. Add the chicken thighs and allow the stock to come back to almost boiling point again.

- Reduce the heat to low, partially cover the pan with a lid and simmer the chicken thighs for 25 minutes. Remove the cooked chicken thighs from the stock and set aside on a plate to cool completely.

- At this stage the chicken is ready to use as per your chosen recipe. Alternatively, let it cool completely and keep it in the fridge for up to 2 days, or freeze for up to 3 months. Defrost the chicken before using in recipe dishes.

Tip: The leftover stock used to cook the chicken is full of flavour – add some soft noodles or shredded chicken with sliced vegetables and enjoy it as a soup!

CRISPY CHICKEN

Makes enough crispy chicken for 3 main dishes (about 40 pieces of crispy chicken)

½ teaspoon sea salt
½ teaspoon MSG
¼ teaspoon ground white pepper
¼ teaspoon Chinese 5-spice
1 teaspoon rice wine
2 large skinless, boneless chicken breast fillets (300–350g total weight), diced or thinly sliced
1 egg
5 tablespoons potato starch
5 tablespoons custard powder (original, not instant)
Oil for deep-frying

- Put the sea salt, MSG, white pepper, Chinese 5-spice and rice wine in a bowl and mix. Add the diced or sliced chicken breast and mix well. Set aside for 5 minutes.

- Add the egg to the prepared bowl of chicken and mix well once more. In a separate bowl, combine the potato starch and custard powder. Heat the oil for deep-frying to 180°C/350°F.

- Working in batches, transfer some of the prepared chicken into the bowl of flour and custard powder and mix well. Don't worry if the chicken pieces aren't completely coated in flour – the sticky egg/flour coating will crisp up during cooking. Shake off any excess flour and carefully drop the coated chicken pieces into the hot oil. Fry for 3–4 minutes, or until the chicken is cooked through and the coating is just a little coloured. Use a slotted spoon to remove the chicken from the oil, drain off any excess oil and set aside on a plate. Repeat the process until all the crispy chicken is cooked.

- At this stage the chicken is ready to use as per your chosen recipe. Alternatively, let it cool completely and keep it in the fridge for up to 2 days, or freeze for up to 3 months.

- To reheat the crispy chicken: heat the oil for deep-frying and fry the chicken pieces for 2–3 minutes (fresh) or 3–4 minutes (frozen) until heated through.

- This chicken can be used for Cantonese-style Sweet and Sour Chicken (page 136) or Salt and Chilli Chicken (page 90), or combine it with any of your favourite stir-fry sauces.

CHICKEN BALLS

Serves 1

250g self-raising flour
½ teaspoon sea salt
½ teaspoon MSG
Pinch of ground white pepper
225–275ml cold water
Oil for deep-frying
1 skinless, boneless chicken breast fillet (about 150g), cut
  into 7–8 pieces

- Combine the self-raising flour, sea salt, MSG and white pepper in a large bowl. Gradually add the water, whisking well until a thick batter is formed. Add more water if the batter is too thick, or more flour if the batter is too thin.

- Heat the oil for deep-frying to 170°C/340°F. Dip each chicken piece in the batter until fully coated, drop carefully into the hot oil and fry for about 5 minutes or until the chicken balls are cooked through, crispy and golden.

- Remove from the oil using a slotted spoon, drain off any excess oil and arrange the chicken balls on a plate lined with kitchen paper. Serve with Sweet and Sour Sauce (page 200).

- At this stage the chicken is ready to use as per your chosen recipe. Alternatively, let it cool completely and keep it in the fridge for up to 2 days, or freeze for up to 3 months.

- To reheat, fry the (defrosted if frozen) chicken balls again in hot oil (170°C/340°F) for 2–3 minutes or until piping hot throughout (internal temperature of 75°C/165°F or above).

CRISPY PORK

Makes enough crispy pork for 3 main dishes

300g pork tenderloin fillet, diced or thinly sliced
½ teaspoon sea salt
½ teaspoon MSG
¼ teaspoon ground white pepper
¼ teaspoon Chinese 5-spice
1 teaspoon rice wine
1 egg
5 tablespoons potato starch
5 tablespoons custard powder (original, not instant)
Oil for deep-frying

- Put the diced or sliced pork, sea salt, MSG, white pepper, Chinese 5-spice and rice wine in a bowl, mix well and set aside for 10 minutes. Add the egg and mix well once more.

- Combine the potato starch and custard powder in a large bowl.

- Heat the oil for deep-frying to 180°C/350°F.

- Working in batches, transfer some of the pork into the bowl of flour and custard powder and mix well. Don't worry if the pork pieces aren't completely coated in flour – the sticky egg/flour coating will crisp up during cooking. Shake off any excess flour and carefully drop the coated pork pieces into the hot oil. Fry for 3–4 minutes, or until the pork is cooked through and the coating is just a little coloured. Use a slotted spoon to remove the pork from the oil, drain off any excess oil and set aside on a plate. Repeat the process until all the crispy pork is cooked.

- At this stage the pork is ready to eat or use as per your chosen recipe. Alternatively, let it cool completely and keep it in the fridge for up to 2 days, or freeze for up to 3 months.

- To reheat the crispy pork: heat oil for deep-frying and fry the pork pieces for 2–3 minutes (fresh) or 3–4 minutes (frozen) until heated through.

- Tip: Add the crispy pork pieces to your favourite stir-fry sauce or use for the Salt and Chilli Crispy Pork (page 90).

PORK BALLS

Serves 1

250g self-raising flour
½ teaspoon sea salt
½ teaspoon MSG
Pinch of ground white pepper
225–275ml cold water
Oil for deep-frying
175g pork tenderloin fillet, cut into 7 or 8 pieces

- Put the self-raising flour, sea salt, MSG and white pepper in a large bowl, mix briefly, then gradually add the water, whisking well until a thick batter is formed. Add more water if the batter is too thick, or more flour if the batter is too thin.

- Heat the oil for deep-frying to 170°C/340°F. Dip each pork piece in the batter until fully coated, drop carefully into the hot oil and fry for about 5 minutes, or until the pork balls are cooked through, crispy and golden.

- Remove from the oil using a slotted spoon, drain off any excess oil and arrange the pork balls on a plate lined with kitchen paper. Serve with Sweet and Sour Sauce (page 200).

- At this stage the pork is ready to use as per your chosen recipe. Alternatively, let it cool completely and keep it in the fridge for up to 2 days, or freeze for up to 3 months.

- To reheat, fry the (defrosted if frozen) pork balls again in hot oil (170°C/340°F) for 2–3 minutes or until piping hot throughout (internal temperature of 75°C/165°F or above).

CHAR SIU PORK

Makes enough pork for 3–4 main dishes or 8–10 smaller soups

This recipe uses pork tenderloin; however, pork, shoulder can be used with good results.

1 tablespoon golden syrup
1 tablespoon rice wine
2 teaspoons light soy sauce
1 teaspoon dark soy sauce
3 tablespoons hoisin sauce
2 tablespoons tomato ketchup
¼ teaspoon Chinese 5-spice
½ teaspoon smoked garlic powder
½ teaspoon MSG
¼ teaspoon beetroot powder
½ teaspoon sesame oil
2 tablespoons water
1 pork tenderloin fillet (500–600g)

Glaze
½ teaspoon beetroot powder
2 tablespoons golden syrup
1 tablespoon water

- Put the golden syrup, rice wine, light soy sauce, dark soy sauce, hoisin sauce, tomato ketchup, Chinese 5-spice, smoked garlic powder, MSG, beetroot powder, sesame oil and water in a large container and mix well.

- Prod the pork tenderloin a few times with the tip of a sharp knife. Add the pork to the prepared marinade and mix well. Cover and set aside in the fridge overnight, turning the pork fillet once or twice during this time.

- Remove the pork from the fridge 20 minutes before cooking. Preheat the oven to 180°C/Gas 4. Pour 100ml of water into a roasting tray and place the marinated pork fillet on a rack above the tray. Bake the pork in the oven for 15 minutes.

- Combine the glaze ingredients in a bowl. Mix well and brush generously on the char siu pork. Return the pork to the oven and bake for a further 10–15 minutes until the pork is sizzling and the internal temperature measures 75°C or above. If desired, the pork can be finished under a hot grill for 2 minutes to set the glaze further.

- Remove the pork from the oven, cover loosely with foil and leave to rest for 20 minutes.

- The pork is now ready to eat. Alternatively, let it cool completely and keep it in the fridge for up to 2 days, or freeze for up to 3 months.

MARINATED BEEF

This simple marinade uses bicarbonate of soda to tenderise the beef before flavouring it with additional ingredients – this technique is common in Chinese takeaways and is useful for preparing in advance and freezing for future use.

Makes enough marinated beef for 8–10 main dishes

1.5kg topside beef (trimmed weight)
50–75ml cold water
1½ teaspoons bicarbonate of soda
1 tablespoon dark soy sauce
2 teaspoons rice wine
1 teaspoon ground white pepper
2–3 tablespoons potato starch
1 teaspoon sesame oil
2 tablespoons vegetable oil

- Slice the beef thinly against the grain – as you slice the beef, give each slice a hard slap with the back of a large knife to increase the size of each slice (this will also help to tenderise the meat). Put the sliced beef in a large bowl and add the water. Add the bicarbonate of soda and mix well. Cover and set aside in the fridge for 1 hour 20 minutes.

- Mix the sliced beef well (it should have absorbed some of the water by now), add the dark soy sauce, rice wine and white pepper. Add two tablespoons of the potato starch and mix well. Mix once more and the meat should absorb the marinade – add another tablespoon of potato starch if the mix appears wet.

- The meat is now ready to use or can be divided into 180–200g portions and refrigerated or frozen. The sliced marinated beef will keep well in the fridge for up to 2 days or in the freezer for up to 3 months. Defrost portions of marinated beef in the fridge overnight before cooking.

- To cook: heat a wok or large frying pan over a medium-high heat. Add 2 tablespoons of vegetable oil, swirl it around the pan and add a portion of sliced marinated beef. Let the beef cook untouched in the pan for 30 seconds to sear, then stir-fry for 2 minutes until nicely coloured and just cooked through. Add the cooked beef to your favourite stir-fry dishes or curry as per your chosen recipe.

MARINATED STEAK

Makes 1 portion

1 sirloin or rib-eye steak (about 225g)
¼ teaspoon sea salt
¼ teaspoon MSG
Pinch of ground white pepper
½ teaspoon dark soy sauce
1 teaspoon rice wine
1 tablespoon potato starch
1 tablespoon cold water
Dash of sesame oil
1 tablespoon vegetable oil

- Trim any excess fat from the steak and slice it thinly against the grain. Combine the sea salt, MSG, white pepper, dark soy sauce, rice wine, potato starch and water in a bowl. Add the sliced steak and mix well. Set aside for 5 minutes. Add the sesame oil and vegetable oil and mix well once more.

- Heat a wok or large frying pan over a medium to high heat. Add the marinated beef and let it cook untouched in the pan for 30 seconds to sear, then stir-fry for 1–2 minutes until nicely coloured and just cooked through. Add the cooked steak to your favourite stir-fry dishes or curry as per your chosen recipe.

CRISPY BEEF

Makes 1 portion

> 100g beef steak such as thin cut, sirloin or rib-eye
>   (trimmed weight)
> ¼ teaspoon sea salt
> ¼ teaspoon MSG
> Pinch of ground white pepper
> ½ teaspoon rice wine
> 1 egg
> 5 tablespoons potato starch
> 5 tablespoons custard powder (original, not instant)
> Oil for deep-frying

- Cut the beef steak into thin strips against the grain. Put the beef, sea salt, MSG, white pepper and rice wine in a bowl, mix well and set aside for 5 minutes. Beat the egg in a separate bowl and add just enough to coat the marinated beef (the remaining egg can be used for egg-fried rice dishes).

- Put the potato starch and custard powder in a large bowl and mix briefly.

- Heat the oil for deep-frying to 180°C/350°F.

- Place the marinated beef strips into the starch mix and mix well, pressing down hard to ensure the beef is coated. Carefully drop the coated beef pieces into the hot oil and fry for about 5 minutes, or until the beef is crispy and golden. Remove from the oil with a slotted spoon and place on a plate lined with kitchen paper to soak up the excess oil. Add the cooked crispy beef to your favourite stir-fry dishes or curry as per your chosen recipe.

- Alternatively, let it cool completely and keep it in the fridge for up to 2 days, or freeze for up to 3 months.

- To reheat, fry the crispy beef (you can fry it from frozen) again in hot oil (170°C/340°F) for 2–3 minutes or until piping hot throughout.

CRISPY TOFU

This crispy tofu will work well in any of your favourite stir-fry sauces and is also delicious salt and chilli style!

Makes 1 portion

150g extra-firm tofu
5 tablespoons potato starch
5 tablespoons custard powder (original, not instant)
Pinch of sea salt
Pinch of MSG
Oil for deep-frying

- Drain the tofu and use a tofu press to remove the excess water. If you don't have a tofu press, wrap the tofu in kitchen paper and squeeze it gently to remove the excess water. Cut the tofu into small dice and set aside.

- Put the potato starch, custard powder, sea salt and MSG in a bowl and mix well. Heat the oil for deep-frying to 180°C/350°F.

- Working in batches, put the diced tofu into the prepared starch-and-custard-powder mix, pressing down well to ensure the tofu pieces are well coated. Shake off any excess flour and carefully drop the tofu into the hot oil. Fry for about 5 minutes or until the tofu is crispy. Remove from the oil with a slotted spoon and set aside on a plate lined with kitchen paper. Repeat the process until all the tofu is fried.

- The tofu is now ready to add to your favourite stir-fry dishes. The cooked tofu will keep well in the fridge for up to 2 days and can be reheated in a 180°C/Gas 4 oven for 10–12 minutes or fried again in hot oil for 2 minutes until piping hot.

- I have found that tofu doesn't freeze well so I would only advise keeping it in the fridge.

COOKED KING PRAWNS

Makes 1 portion

165g raw shelled king prawns
¼ teaspoon sea salt
¼ teaspoon MSG
1 teaspoon potato starch
1 tablespoon vegetable oil

- Put the king prawns, sea salt, MSG, potato starch and vegetable oil in a bowl, mix well and set aside for 5 minutes.

- Heat a wok or large frying pan over a medium to high heat. Add the prawns and stir-fry for 2–3 minutes or until they are nicely coloured and just cooked through. Add the cooked king prawns to your favourite stir-fry dishes or curry as per your chosen recipe.

CRISPY KING PRAWNS

Makes 1 portion

165g raw shelled king prawns
¼ teaspoon sea salt
¼ teaspoon MSG
1 egg
5 tablespoons potato starch
5 tablespoons custard powder (original, not instant)
Oil for deep-frying

- Put the king prawns, sea salt and MSG in a bowl and mix well. Beat the egg in a separate bowl and add just enough to coat the king prawns (the remaining egg can be used for egg-fried rice dishes). Mix well.

- Put the potato starch and custard powder in a bowl and mix well. Heat the oil for deep-frying to 180°C/350°F.

- Working in batches, transfer some of the prepared prawns into the bowl of flour and custard powder mix and stir well. Don't worry if the prawns aren't completely coated in flour – the sticky egg/flour coating will crisp up during cooking. Shake off any excess flour and carefully drop the coated prawns into the hot oil. Fry for 3–4 minutes or until the prawns are cooked through and the coating is just a little coloured. Use a slotted spoon to remove the prawns from the oil, drain off any excess oil and set aside on a plate.

Repeat the process until all the crispy king prawns are cooked.

- Now the prawns are ready to use as per your chosen recipe.

KING PRAWN BALLS

Makes 1 portion

250g self-raising flour
½ teaspoon sea salt
½ teaspoon MSG
Pinch of ground white pepper
225–275ml cold water
Oil for deep-frying
165g raw shelled king prawns

- Put the self-raising flour, sea salt, MSG and white pepper in a bowl and mix briefly, then gradually add the water, whisking well until a thick batter is formed. Add more water if the batter is too thick, or more flour if the batter is too thin.

- Heat the oil for deep-frying to 170°C/340°F. Dip each king prawn in the batter until fully coated, then drop carefully into the hot oil and fry for about 5 minutes, or until the king prawn balls are cooked through, crispy and golden.

- Remove the king prawn balls from the oil using a slotted spoon, drain off any excess oil and place on a plate lined with kitchen paper. Serve with Sweet Chilli Dipping Sauce (page 202).

STARTERS

When browsing a Chinese takeaway menu in anticipation of placing an order, I'm often convinced that I could happily eat an entire meal made up only of starter dishes. Crispy chicken wings, sticky pork ribs in barbecue sauce, prawn toast, satay skewers, noodle soups . . . choosing just one is a difficult task.

Soups are an ideal way to easily bulk out a meal, especially if cooking for several people, while sharing bowls of savoury, spicy and sweet appetisers will have your guests eagerly awaiting the main course. Variety is the spice of life, so this chapter includes a wide selection of popular starter dishes including all the ones mentioned above.

Many Chinese takeaway restaurants offer a selection of siu mai, which are Chinese-style steamed dumplings. When stocking up on ingredients at your local Chinese supermarket, be sure to check out the freezer aisle where you'll find many good-quality brands of ready-to-cook Chinese dumplings. Typically, these frozen siu mai take just 10 minutes or so to steam-cook, adding another dimension to your homemade feast!

LARGE PANCAKE ROLLS

Makes 4 large pancake rolls

2 teaspoons vegetable oil
½ large onion, thinly sliced
6 button mushrooms, thinly sliced
1 large handful beansprouts (about 150g)
½ teaspoon sea salt
½ teaspoon MSG
Pinch of ground white pepper
Pinch of ground black pepper
1 generous teaspoon Chinese 5-spice
2 teaspoons rice wine
1 tablespoon cold water
1 portion cooked chicken, beef, char siu pork, king prawns or tofu (as desired)
8 large square frozen spring-roll wrappers, defrosted
1 tablespoon potato starch mixed with 1 tablespoon cold water
Oil for deep-frying

- Heat a wok or large frying pan over a medium to high heat. Add the vegetable oil, then add the sliced onion and mushrooms and stir-fry for 2 minutes. Add the beansprouts and stir-fry for a further 1 minute.

- Add the sea salt, MSG, white pepper, black pepper, Chinese

5-spice and rice wine. Stir-fry for 2 minutes, then add the cold water and stir-fry for another 1 minute. Transfer the stir-fried vegetables to a colander to drain off any excess liquid and set aside to cool completely. Add the cooked chicken, beef, char siu pork or king prawns to the mix, if using.

- Heat the oil for deep-frying to 180°C/350°F.

- Arrange two spring-roll wrappers slightly overlapping on a work surface with one corner of the bottom square of wrapper closest to you. Brush the top of the wrappers with the potato starch-and-water mix and place about 4 generous tablespoons of filling mixture in the lower third of the arranged wrappers. Fold them up from the bottom over the filling, then fold in the sides and continue rolling to form the spring roll, pressing down gently to seal with more of the potato starch-and-water mixture. Cover with a clean, damp tea towel and repeat the process with the remaining spring-roll wrappers and mixture.

- Carefully add the prepared pancake rolls to the hot oil and fry for 4–5 minutes, turning them occasionally, until golden and crispy. Remove the pancake rolls from the oil with a slotted spoon and set aside on a plate lined with kitchen paper to soak up any excess oil. Serve with Sweet and Sour Sauce (page 200).

CRISPY CHICKEN WINGS

Serves about 4 (24 wings in total, depending on size)

1kg chicken wings, wing tips removed
1 teaspoon rice wine
½ teaspoon Chinese 5-spice
½ teaspoon smoked garlic powder
½ teaspoon sea salt
½ teaspoon MSG
½ teaspoon ground black pepper
¼ teaspoon ground white pepper
1 egg
250g plain flour
Oil for deep-frying

- Joint the chicken wings using a sharp knife to separate the drumettes and wingettes. Put all the wing pieces in a large bowl and add the rice wine, Chinese 5-spice, smoked garlic powder, sea salt, MSG, black pepper and white pepper. Mix well and set aside for 5 minutes.

- Add the egg to the prepared chicken wings and mix well. Put the plain flour in a separate large bowl.

- Heat the oil for deep-frying to 180°C/350°F. Working in batches, press some of the chicken wings into the plain flour, mixing well and pressing down hard until the wings are fully coated. Carefully drop the coated chicken wings into the hot oil and fry for about 10 minutes or until just cooked through and golden. Use a slotted spoon to remove the chicken wings from the oil, drain off any excess oil and set aside on a plate. Repeat the process until all the chicken wings are coated and cooked.

- The wings can be eaten immediately or set aside to cool completely and stored in the fridge for up to 2 days or in the freezer for up to 3 months. They are delicious as they are, or you can take them to another level by coating them generously with Chinese-style BBQ Sauce (page 206) or Sweet and Sour Sauce (page 200).

- To reheat the crispy chicken wings (defrosted if frozen), heat the oil for deep-frying to 180°C/350°F and re-fry the wings for 3 minutes until piping hot, or bake them in a 180°C/350°F oven for 10–12 minutes.

Variation:
Salt and Chilli Chicken Wings (page 92).

SWEET SESAME CHICKEN BITES

Serves 1

1 tablespoon white sesame seeds
2 tablespoons tomato ketchup
1 tablespoon sweet chilli sauce (shop-bought or use my
   recipe on page 201)
1 tablespoon golden syrup
1 tablespoon dark brown sugar
2 teaspoons rice wine vinegar
2 teaspoons light soy sauce
½ teaspoon dark soy sauce
1 generous teaspoon chopped Garlic in Oil (page 211)
1 tablespoon water
1 portion cooked Crispy Chicken (page 28)
1 spring onion, thinly sliced, to serve

- Heat a dry wok or frying pan over a medium heat, add the sesame seeds and toast for 2–3 minutes until golden and aromatic. Tip into a small bowl and set aside.

- Put the tomato ketchup, sweet chilli sauce, golden syrup, brown sugar, rice wine vinegar, light soy sauce, dark soy sauce, chopped garlic and water in a pan and mix briefly. Heat over a medium to high heat until the sauce starts to boil, then reduce the heat to low and simmer for 2–3 minutes, or until the sauce reduces and is thick and syrupy.

- Toss the crispy fried chicken pieces in the sauce and mix gently until all the crispy chicken is coated. Transfer to a serving bowl, sprinkle with the toasted sesame seeds and spring onion, and serve.

FRIED PORK SPARE RIBS

Serves 1

The first cooking step in making these ribs involves a long, slow simmer – ideal for a lazy Sunday afternoon. With the ribs cooked and cooled, you're just minutes away from a feast! Save the leftover cooking liquid and use it to make the Chinese-style BBQ Sauce (page 206) or Peking Sauce (page 204).

800g pork spare ribs
1 whole star anise
¼ teaspoon sea salt
¼ teaspoon MSG
1 teaspoon caster sugar
¼ teaspoon Chinese 5-spice
1 teaspoon smoked garlic powder
1 teaspoon beetroot powder
2 tablespoons hoisin sauce
1 tablespoon tomato ketchup
1 teaspoon rice wine
1 litre water
Oil for deep-frying

- Put the pork ribs in a large saucepan, cover completely with water and set aside for 20 minutes. Drain the water and return the pork ribs to the pan.

- Add the star anise, sea salt, MSG, caster sugar, Chinese 5-spice, smoked garlic powder, beetroot powder, hoisin sauce, tomato ketchup, rice wine and water. Mix well. Bring to the boil, reduce the heat to low and cover almost completely with a lid.

- Simmer the pork ribs for 1 hour 50 minutes, or until the pork meat is tender but not quite falling off the bone. Using tongs, remove the cooked spare ribs from the liquid and set aside on a plate to cool. When cool, cover and set aside in the fridge until needed (the cooked ribs will keep well in the fridge for up to 2 days, or in the freezer for up to 3 months).

- Allow the cooking liquid to cool completely. This liquid is now pork stock and can be used to make the Chinese-style BBQ Sauce (page 206) or Peking Sauce (page 204). If you'd like to keep the stock for making sauces, divide it into 150ml portions in food-safe bags or containers. This pork stock will keep in the fridge for up to 2 days or in the freezer for up to 3 months.

- To finish the ribs (defrosted if frozen), heat the oil for deep-frying to 160°C/320°F. Carefully add the ribs to the hot oil in batches and fry for about 5 minutes until the ribs are piping hot and just beginning to crisp up around the edges, turning the ribs occasionally. Increase the oil temperature to 180°C/350°F and fry the ribs for a further 2 minutes until nicely coloured and slightly crisp. Repeat until all the ribs are fried.

- Remove the ribs from the oil using tongs. Serve plain, or drenched in Chinese-style BBQ Sauce (page 206) or Peking Sauce (page 204).

SALT AND CHILLI BONELESS RIBS

Serves 1

Using a cooking technique similar to that used in the Thai dish *moo dad deaw*, pork tenderloin fillet is slowly dried and then quickly flash-fried. The result is a rib-like texture to the meat, hence the name I've chosen for this dish.

300g pork tenderloin fillet
½ teaspoon dark brown sugar
Pinch of ground white pepper
½ teaspoon oyster sauce
2 teaspoons water
Oil for deep-frying
1 tablespoon vegetable oil
¼ large onion, thinly sliced
1 generous teaspoon chopped Garlic in Oil (page 211)
1 teaspoon Salt and Pepper Seasoning (page 214), or to taste
1 spring onion, thinly sliced
½ teaspoon dried chilli flakes
1 tablespoon rice wine

- Cut the pork fillet into 1.5cm-thick slices. Put the sliced pork in a bowl and add the dark brown sugar, white pepper, oyster sauce and water. Mix well and set aside for 10 minutes.

- Heat the oven to its lowest setting, ideally about 80°C/ lowest Gas. If your oven has a 'keep warm' setting, use this instead. Arrange the sliced pork on a wire rack set over a baking tray and bake for 1 hour.

- Heat the oil for deep-frying to 180°C/350°F. Carefully drop the dried pork pieces into the hot oil in batches and fry for 1–2 minutes, or until the pork is nicely coloured and crispy. Remove from the oil with a slotted spoon and set aside on a plate. Repeat the process until all the pork pieces are fried.

- Heat a wok or large frying pan over a medium to high heat. Add 1 tablespoon vegetable oil, then add the sliced onion and stir-fry for 30–40 seconds. Add the fried pork, chopped garlic in oil and salt and pepper seasoning. Stir-fry well for 30 seconds, then add the spring onion, dried chilli flakes and rice wine, mix well once more, remove from the heat and serve.

CRISPY WONTON

Serves 1 (makes 8 crispy wontons)

165g raw shelled king prawns, finely chopped
¼ teaspoon sea salt
Pinch of MSG
Pinch of caster sugar
Pinch of ground white pepper
Pinch of ground black pepper
Pinch of Chinese 5-spice
½ teaspoon oyster sauce
½ teaspoon chopped Garlic in Oil (page 211)
Dash of sesame oil
Dash of rice wine
1 teaspoon potato starch
8 wonton wrappers, defrosted if frozen
Oil for deep-frying

- Put the chopped king prawns in a large bowl. Add the sea salt, MSG, sugar, white pepper, black pepper, Chinese 5-spice, oyster sauce, chopped garlic in oil, sesame oil, rice wine and potato starch, mix well and set aside for 10 minutes.

- Place a small amount of the mixture into the middle of a wonton wrapper. Twist the top firmly to create a seal. Cover with a clean, damp tea towel and repeat the process with the remaining wonton wrappers and filling.

- Heat the oil for deep-frying to 165°C/330°F. Gently drop the wontons into the hot oil and fry for about 5 minutes, or until golden and crispy. Remove from the oil with a slotted spoon, arrange on a plate lined with kitchen paper to drain off any excess oil and serve with Sweet Chilli Sauce (page 202).

SESAME KING PRAWNS

Serves 1

125g self-raising flour
Pinch of sea salt
Pinch of MSG
100–150ml cold water
165g raw shelled king prawns
Oil for deep-frying
2 tablespoons golden syrup
1 tablespoon toasted white sesame seeds

- Put the self-raising flour, sea salt and MSG in a bowl and mix briefly, then gradually add the water (you may not need all the water), whisking well until a thick batter is formed. Add more water if the batter is too thick, or more flour if the batter is too thin.

- Heat oil for deep-frying to 170°C/340°F. Dip each king prawn into the batter until fully coated then drop them carefully into the hot oil and fry for about 5 minutes or until the king prawns are cooked through and the batter is crisp and golden. Remove the king prawns from the oil using a slotted spoon, drain off any excess oil and arrange on a plate lined with kitchen paper.

- Place the king prawns on a serving plate and generously drizzle with golden syrup. Sprinkle with the toasted sesame seeds and serve.

SESAME PRAWN TOAST

Makes about 16 slices (64 pieces)

This hugely popular side dish is so simple to make and will live in your freezer quite happily for up to 3 months, ready to be fried from frozen in just a few minutes!

Prawn mixture
  320g fresh (not frozen) raw king prawns
  1 egg
  ¼ teaspoon sea salt
  ¼ teaspoon MSG
  ¼ teaspoon caster sugar
  ¼ teaspoon ground white pepper
  ¼ teaspoon ground black pepper
  ¼ teaspoon Chinese 5-spice
  1 teaspoon oyster sauce
  Dash of fish sauce
  ½ teaspoon sesame oil
  1 tablespoon chopped Garlic in Oil (page 211)
  1 tablespoon rice wine
  1 tablespoon water
  1 teaspoon potato starch

Toasts
  2 x 400g 'toastie'-style white bread loaves (or any other thick white bread)

250g white sesame seeds
Oil for deep-frying

- Put the raw king prawns, egg, sea salt, MSG, sugar, white pepper, black pepper, Chinese 5-spice, oyster sauce, fish sauce, sesame oil, garlic in oil, rice wine, water and potato starch in a blender and blend to a smooth paste.

- Using a flat spatula, spread about 2 teaspoons of the prepared prawn mix onto a bread slice, spreading it all the way to the edges of the bread. Pour the sesame seeds onto a large plate and press the bread, prawn side down, firmly into the sesame seeds to coat. Flip the prepared prawn toast slice over, cut into 4 triangles and arrange on a sheet of baking paper.

- Repeat the process with the remaining prawn mix and bread until all the mix is used up, layering the prawn toast slices between sheets of baking paper. Open-freeze for 6 hours or overnight, then transfer the frozen prawn toast slices to a freezer-safe food bag.

- To cook the prawn toasts, heat the oil for deep-frying to 165°C/330°F. Carefully place some of the frozen king prawn slices into the hot oil with the prawn and sesame side facing down and fry for 2½ minutes. Carefully flip the prawn toasts over with tongs and fry for another 2 minutes, or until the toast is golden and crispy. Remove the toasts from the oil with tongs and arrange on a plate lined with kitchen paper. Repeat until all your toasts are fried. Serve with Sweet Chilli Sauce (page 202) or Sweet and Sour Sauce (page 200).

SESAME CHICKEN TOAST

Makes about 16 slices (64 pieces)

Chicken mixture

- 2 large skinless, boneless chicken breast fillets (about 300g total weight – as the toasts will be frozen, it's important to use chicken which hasn't previously been frozen)
- 1 egg white
- ¼ teaspoon sea salt
- ¼ teaspoon MSG
- ¼ teaspoon caster sugar
- ¼ teaspoon ground white pepper
- ¼ teaspoon ground black pepper
- ¼ teaspoon Chinese 5-spice
- 1 teaspoon oyster sauce
- ½ teaspoon sesame oil
- 1 tablespoon chopped Garlic in Oil (page 211)
- 1 tablespoon rice wine
- 1 tablespoon water
- 2 teaspoons potato starch

Toasts

- 2 x 400g 'toastie'-style white bread loaves (or any other thick white bread)
- 250g white sesame seeds
- Oil for deep-frying

- Trim any excess fat from the chicken breast fillets and cut the fillets into small pieces. Put the chicken breast pieces, egg white, sea salt, MSG, sugar, white pepper, black pepper, Chinese 5-spice, oyster sauce, sesame oil, garlic in oil, rice wine, water and potato starch in a blender and blend to a smooth paste.

- Using a flat spatula, spread around 2 teaspoons of the prepared chicken mix onto a bread slice, spreading it all the way to the edges of the bread. Pour the sesame seeds onto a large plate and press the bread, chicken side down, firmly into the sesame seeds to coat. Flip the prepared chicken toast slice over, cut into 4 triangles and arrange on a sheet of baking paper.

- Repeat the process with the remaining chicken mix and bread until all the mix is used up, layering the chicken toast slices between sheets of baking paper. Open-freeze for 6 hours or overnight, then transfer the chicken toast slices to a freezer-safe food bag.

- To cook the chicken toasts, heat the oil for deep-frying to 165°C/330°F. Carefully place some of the frozen chicken toast slices into the hot oil with the chicken and sesame side facing down and fry for 3 minutes. Carefully flip the chicken toasts over with tongs and fry for another 2 minutes, or until the toast is golden and crispy. Remove the toasts from the oil with tongs and arrange on a plate lined with kitchen paper. Repeat until all your toasts are fried. Serve with Sweet Chilli Sauce (page 202) or Sweet and Sour Sauce (page 200).

CHICKEN SATAY SKEWERS

Serves 1 (makes 6 skewers)

Chicken marinade
- ½ teaspoon light soy sauce
- ½ teaspoon dark soy sauce
- ½ teaspoon chicken powder
- ¼ teaspoon curry powder (I recommend using Eastern Star or 'Madras style' curry powder)
- ½ teaspoon Jimmy's saté sauce
- 2 teaspoons potato starch
- 1 skinless, boneless chicken breast fillet, sliced into 6 strips

Skewers and vegetables
- 6 small bamboo skewers
- Oil, for shallow- or deep-frying
- ¼ onion, roughly chopped
- ¼ green pepper, deseeded and roughly chopped
- 1 portion Satay Sauce (page 203), to serve

- Put the light soy sauce, dark soy sauce, chicken powder, curry powder, saté sauce and potato starch in a bowl. Add the chicken strips and mix thoroughly until evenly coated. Cover and set aside in the fridge for at least 1 hour, or overnight.

- Twenty minutes before you want to cook, put your bamboo skewers in cold water and leave them to soak, to prevent them from burning during cooking.

- Heat the oil for frying to 170°C/340°F. A large shallow frying pan works well here and allows several skewers to be fried at the same time. Thread each chicken strip onto a bamboo skewer, piercing the chicken several times to ensure it's securely held on the skewer. Carefully place each chicken skewer into the hot oil and fry for about 3 minutes, or until the chicken skewers are cooked through and nicely coloured. Turn the skewers in the oil occasionally to ensure all the chicken is evenly cooked.

- Remove the skewers from the oil and drain off any excess oil. Briefly fry the chopped onion and pepper in the hot oil for about 20 seconds, remove with a slotted spoon and drain off any excess oil. Arrange the vegetables on a serving plate or takeaway container. Place the cooked chicken skewers on top and serve with satay sauce, either on the side or poured generously over the chicken skewers.

FILLET OF BEEF SATAY SKEWERS

Serves 1 (makes 7 skewers)

Beef marinade
¼ teaspoon sea salt
Pinch of MSG
½ teaspoon light soy sauce
½ teaspoon dark soy sauce
¼ teaspoon curry powder (I recommend Eastern Star or 'Madras-style' curry powder)
½ teaspoon Jimmy's saté sauce
1 tablespoon potato starch
1 beef fillet steak (about 170g), sliced against the grain into 7 strips

Skewers and vegetables
7 small bamboo skewers
Oil, for shallow- or deep-frying
¼ onion, roughly chopped
¼ green pepper, deseeded and roughly chopped
1 portion Satay Sauce (page 203), to serve

- Put the sea salt, MSG, light soy sauce, dark soy sauce, curry powder, saté sauce and potato starch in a bowl. Add the beef strips and mix thoroughly until evenly coated. Cover and set aside in the fridge for at least 1 hour, or overnight.

- Twenty minutes before you want to cook, put your bamboo skewers in cold water and leave them to soak, to prevent them from burning during cooking. Take the marinated beef out of the fridge at this stage too, and leave at room temperature for 20 minutes.

- Heat the oil for frying to 180°C/350°F. A large shallow frying pan works well here and allows several skewers to be fried at the same time. Thread each beef strip onto a bamboo skewer, piercing the beef several times to ensure that it's securely held on the skewer. Carefully place each beef skewer into the hot oil and fry for about 2 minutes, or until the beef is nicely charred on the outside and still medium doneness in the centre (cook them for a further minute if you prefer the meat to be well done).

- Remove the skewers from the oil and drain off any excess oil. Briefly fry the chopped onion and pepper in the hot oil for about 20 seconds, remove with a slotted spoon and drain off any excess oil. Arrange the vegetables on a serving plate or takeaway container. Place the cooked beef skewers on top and serve with satay sauce, either on the side or poured generously over the beef skewers.

YUK SUNG (CHINESE-STYLE LETTUCE WRAPS)

Serves 1–2

If you're a fan of Thai laab dishes, you're sure to enjoy this minced pork or chicken in a savoury and sweet sauce, delivered with a burst of freshness thanks to the lettuce leaves. This dish is often served topped with crispy vermicelli noodles – to add these to your dish, heat oil for deep-frying to 190°C/375°F and add a small handful of vermicelli rice noodles. The noodles should immediately puff up – remove from the oil with a slotted spoon and set aside on kitchen paper before garnishing your lettuce wraps.

1 teaspoon vegetable oil
¼ large onion, finely chopped
¼ carrot, finely chopped
1 button mushroom, finely chopped
1–2 pieces of tinned bamboo shoots (optional), finely chopped
125g pork mince (or 125g boneless, skinless chicken thigh, very finely chopped)
1 teaspoon chopped Garlic in Oil (page 211)
1 teaspoon rice wine
Dash of sesame oil
1 spring onion, thinly sliced
4–6 Little Gem lettuce leaves or iceberg lettuce leaves
1 teaspoon white toasted sesame seeds (optional)

Sauce

    2 teaspoons oyster sauce

    2 teaspoons light soy sauce

    1 teaspoon dark soy sauce

    ¼ teaspoon caster sugar

    Pinch of ground white pepper

    ½ teaspoon Chinese 5-spice

    1 teaspoon water

- Put the sauce ingredients in a bowl, mix well and set aside.

- Heat a wok or large frying pan over a medium to high heat. Add the vegetable oil, then add the chopped onion, carrot, mushroom and bamboo shoots and stir-fry for 1 minute. Add the pork mince and stir-fry for 2–3 minutes until the pork is browned and any excess water released has begun to cook off. Add the chopped garlic in oil and mix well. Add the prepared sauce, bring to the boil and simmer for 1 minute or until the sauce has thickened slightly. Add the rice wine, sesame oil and spring onion, and mix through once more.

- Arrange the lettuce leaves on a serving plate and top generously with the prepared pork and sauce. Top with crispy vermicelli noodles or toasted sesame seeds, if using, and serve.

CRISPY SEAWEED

Despite its name, Chinese takeaway-style crispy seaweed is in fact made from what you'll find in supermarkets labelled 'spring greens'. Curly kale will also work well. Traditionally it's topped with a strongly-flavoured ground fried fish (page 14) – if you're not a fan, try topping it with just sugar, or a pinch of Chinese 5-spice.

Serves 1–2

5–6 large fresh green leaves, stalks removed
Oil for deep-frying
½ teaspoon caster sugar
1 teaspoon ground fish

- Roll up the trimmed leaves and shred into fine strips.

- Bring a saucepan of water to the boil. Add the shredded green leaves, stir well and simmer for 30–40 seconds until slightly softened. Drain, rinse with cold water and squeeze tightly to remove the excess water. Separate the leaves out on a plate and set aside to dry for 5 minutes.

- Heat the oil for deep-frying to 185°C/365°F. Carefully drop the shredded green leaves into the hot oil and fry for 30–40 seconds, or until crisp. Remove the crispy leaves from the oil with a slotted spoon and place onto a plate lined with kitchen paper to soak up any excess oil. Transfer the crispy leaves to a plate, add the sugar and mix well. Top with the ground fish and serve.

SIU MAI

If you're lucky enough to live near a large-sized Chinese supermarket with a freezer aisle, you'll most likely find a wide range of frozen siu mai (Chinese dumplings), which you can easily fry or steam at home. While some restaurants may make their dumplings from scratch (and you should definitely order some if your local restaurant does), it's likely that the siu mai you'll find in Chinese supermarkets will be the very same product used by takeaways.

• To cook your siu mai at home you'll need a steamer basket for your wok. Typically, a 10 to 12-minute steam results in delicious dumplings to accompany your feast. Alternatively, frozen siu mai can be fried in oil until heated through and crispy.

SIU MAI DIPPING SAUCE

This simple dip is salty, sweet and full of flavour, and it is perfect to accompany steamed dumplings.

1 tablespoon light soy sauce
1 teaspoon dark soy sauce
1 tablespoon mirin
Pinch of dried chilli flakes
1 generous teaspoon chopped Garlic in Oil (page 211)
1 teaspoon water

- Put the light soy sauce, dark soy sauce, mirin, chilli flakes, garlic in oil and water in a bowl, mix well and serve with steamed dumplings.

SOUPS

A hearty bowl of piping-hot soup is soothing for the soul, particularly in cold winter months. Rich, aromatic broths, soft noodles and the slight kick of heat from white pepper combine to make something truly satisfying.

While the recipes in this chapter are simple at heart, the variety of ways in which you can elaborate or enhance your favourite soups is endless; store-cupboard stock cubes are entirely acceptable, or you can upgrade your broth and make one from scratch yourself (page 218). Whichever method you choose, your meal will only be enhanced by the addition of a comforting bowl of savoury goodness, perhaps even with the spicy addition of homemade chilli oil (page 213).

CHICKEN AND MUSHROOM SOUP

Serves 1

275ml Light Chicken Stock (page 218) or low-salt chicken
    stock from a cube
Dash of light soy sauce
¼ teaspoon dark soy sauce
¼ teaspoon sea salt
¼ teaspoon MSG
Pinch of ground white pepper
40g raw chicken breast fillet, sliced (or 1 small handful
    cooked sliced chicken breast or thigh meat)
3 button mushrooms, very thinly sliced

- Put the light chicken stock, light soy sauce, dark soy sauce,
  sea salt, MSG and white pepper in a saucepan, bring to the
  boil, then reduce to a simmer.

- Add the sliced chicken and sliced mushrooms to the soup
  and simmer for about 3 minutes until the chicken is cooked
  through. Ladle the soup into a serving bowl and serve.

CHICKEN NOODLE SOUP

Serves 1

40g thin wheat noodles (soaked and drained weight) (I
  use the Lucky Boat brand)
275ml Light Chicken Stock (page 218) or low-salt chicken
  stock from a cube
Dash of light soy sauce
¼ teaspoon sea salt
¼ teaspoon MSG
Pinch of ground white pepper
50g raw chicken breast fillet, sliced (or 1 small handful
  cooked sliced chicken breast or thigh meat)

To serve

1 spring onion, very thinly sliced
¼ teaspoon sesame oil (optional)

- Prepare the noodles as described on page 173 and place
  40g of prepared noodles in a soup bowl. Set aside.

- Put the light chicken stock, light soy sauce, sea salt, MSG
  and white pepper in a saucepan, bring to the boil, then
  reduce to a simmer.

- Add the sliced chicken to the soup and simmer for about
  3 minutes until the chicken is cooked through. Pour the chicken
  soup over the prepared noodles in the bowl. Garnish with the
  sliced spring onion, drizzle with sesame oil (if using), and serve.

CHICKEN AND SWEETCORN SOUP

Serves 1

225ml Light Chicken Stock (page 218) or low-salt chicken
stock from a cube
¼ teaspoon sea salt
¼ teaspoon MSG
50g raw chicken breast fillet, sliced (or 1 small handful
cooked sliced chicken breast or thigh meat)
200g tinned creamed corn
1 teaspoon potato starch mixed with 1 tablespoon cold
water
1 egg white, briefly stirred with a fork

- Put the light chicken stock, sea salt and MSG in a saucepan, bring to the boil, then reduce to a simmer.

- Add the sliced chicken to the soup and simmer for about
3 minutes until the chicken is cooked through. Add the
tinned creamed corn and simmer for a further 1 minute.

- Gradually add the starch-and-water mix and stir well until
the soup has thickened slightly (you may not need to use all
the mix). Simmer for 30 seconds. Gradually pour the egg
white into the simmering soup, stirring slowly to create
thin ribbons. Pour into a soup bowl and serve.

HOT AND SOUR SOUP

Hot bean sauce and black vinegar combine to create a deliciously tangy flavour.

Serves 2

Pinch of dried black fungus
1 dried shiitake mushroom
1 egg
Dash of sesame oil
1 teaspoon water
400ml Light Chicken Stock (page 218) or low-salt chicken
    stock from a cube
¼ teaspoon chopped Garlic in Oil (page 211)
Pinch of sea salt
Pinch of MSG
¼ teaspoon caster sugar
1 teaspoon light soy sauce
Dash of dark soy sauce
1½ teaspoons hot bean sauce
1 small handful cooked chicken, char siu pork, king
    prawns or tofu (or a combination of all three)
1 small handful tinned bamboo shoots (rinsed and
    drained) (about 25g), thinly sliced
½ small carrot, thinly sliced
Pinch of ground white pepper
2 teaspoons black vinegar (*chinkiang*)

  2 teaspoons potato starch mixed with 2 tablespoons cold
    water
  1 egg
  1 spring onion, thinly sliced, to serve

- First, prepare the dried fungus and shiitake mushroom. Place the fungus and shiitake mushroom in a heatproof bowl and cover with warm (not boiling) water. Set aside for about 30 minutes, rinse and drain well. Thinly slice the fungus and mushroom and set aside.

- Whisk the egg, sesame oil and water in a bowl and set aside.

- Put the light chicken stock, garlic in oil, sea salt, MSG, sugar, light soy sauce, dark soy sauce and hot bean sauce in a saucepan. Bring to the boil, then reduce to a simmer. Add the handful of cooked chicken, char siu pork, prawns or tofu, then add the bamboo shoots and carrot and mix well. Simmer for 3 minutes.

- Add the white pepper and black vinegar and mix well. Thicken the soup by gradually adding the starch-and-water mix, stirring, until the soup reaches the desired consistency (you may not need to use all the mix). Whisk the egg and slowly pour it into the simmering soup, stirring slowly to create ribbons through the soup. Ladle the hot and sour soup into bowls, garnish with sliced spring onions and serve.

WONTON SOUP

The freezer aisle in your local Chinese supermarket is your best friend when it comes to having ingredients to hand for a quick wonton soup. You could, of course, use vegetable stock and vegetable wontons if you prefer a vegetarian soup.

Serves 1

325ml Light Chicken Stock (page 218) or low-salt chicken
   stock from a cube
Dash of light soy sauce
¼ teaspoon sea salt
¼ teaspoon MSG
Pinch of ground white pepper
5–6 pork and prawn frozen wontons, to taste

To serve
1 spring onion, thinly sliced
Dash of sesame oil (optional)

- Put the light chicken stock, light soy sauce, sea salt, MSG and white pepper in a saucepan. Bring to the boil, add the frozen wontons, bring back to the boil, reduce the heat to medium to low and simmer for about 10 minutes or until the wontons are cooked through.

- Ladle the soup into a serving bowl and garnish with the sliced spring onion. Finish with sesame oil (if using) and serve.

BEEF AND SRIRACHA NOODLE SOUP

Serves 1

40g thin wheat noodles (soaked and drained weight) (I
use the Lucky Boat brand)
275ml Light Chicken Stock (page 218) or low-salt chicken
stock from a cube
Dash of light soy sauce
Dash of dark soy sauce
¼ teaspoon sea salt
¼ teaspoon MSG
Pinch of ground white pepper
½ teaspoon sriracha hot sauce (or to taste)
50g Cooked Beef (page 38 or page 40)

To serve
1 spring onion, thinly sliced
¼ teaspoon sesame oil (optional)

- Prepare the noodles as described in the first step on page
173 and place 40g of prepared noodles in a soup bowl. Set
aside.

- Put the light chicken stock, light soy sauce, dark soy sauce,
sea salt, MSG and white pepper in a saucepan. Bring to the
boil, then reduce to a simmer. Add the sriracha hot sauce
and mix through.

- Add the cooked beef to the soup and simmer for about 3 minutes until the meat is heated through.

- Ladle the soup into the bowl of noodles, garnish with the sliced spring onion, drizzle with the sesame oil (if using) and serve.

TOMATO EGG-DROP SOUP

Serves 1

1 teaspoon vegetable oil

1 large salad tomato, roughly chopped

275ml Light Chicken Stock (page 218), vegetable stock or
water

Dash of light soy sauce

½ teaspoon sea salt

¼ teaspoon MSG

¼ teaspoon caster sugar

Pinch of ground white pepper

1 teaspoon potato starch mixed with 1 tablespoon cold
water

1 egg

1 teaspoon water

1 teaspoon distilled clear malt vinegar

Dash of sesame oil or chopped Garlic in Oil (page 211)
(optional)

1 spring onion, thinly sliced, to serve

- Heat the vegetable oil in a saucepan over a medium heat.
  Add the chopped tomato and stir-fry for 1 minute, then add
  the stock or water, light soy sauce, sea salt, MSG, sugar and
  white pepper. Bring to the boil and simmer for 2 minutes.
  Gradually add the starch-and-water mix, stirring well until
  the soup is thickened slightly (you may not need all the mix).

- Whisk the egg and water together in a bowl. Stir the soup vigorously in a circular motion and slowly pour the whisked egg into the soup. Mix gently for 20–30 seconds until the egg is just cooked and forms ribbons in the soup. Add the vinegar and sesame or garlic in oil, if using. Mix once more, ladle into a soup bowl, garnish with the sliced spring onion and serve.

MIXED VEGETABLE SOUP

Serves 1

325ml Light Chicken Stock (page 218) or vegetable stock
¼ teaspoon sea salt
¼ teaspoon MSG
Dash of light soy sauce
2 baby sweetcorn, each cut into 3 pieces
¼ carrot, thinly sliced
1 button mushroom, thinly sliced
1 small handful tinned bamboo shoots, rinsed and drained
　　(about 25g)
Dash of sesame oil or chopped Garlic in Oil (page 211)
　　(optional)
1 spring onion, thinly sliced, to serve

- Put the light chicken stock or vegetable stock in a saucepan and add the sea salt, MSG and light soy sauce. Bring to the boil, then add the baby sweetcorn and sliced carrot. Simmer for 2 minutes, then add the sliced mushroom and bamboo shoots and simmer for a further 2 minutes.

- Add the sesame oil or garlic in oil, if using, and mix well. Ladle the mixed vegetable soup into a soup bowl, garnish with the sliced spring onion and serve.

SALT AND CHILLI DISHES

In recent years, salt and chilli dishes have become very popular among Chinese takeaway and restaurant customers. Alternatively listed on menus as 'salt & spicy' or 'Jill Yuen style', the aromatic flavour created by the fragrant Salt and Pepper Seasoning (page 214) is utterly delicious, intensified with plentiful amounts of garlic, spring onion and chilli.

Over the years, the salt and chilli finish has been applied to an increasing number of different food items, including a take on the infamous Scottish 'pizza crunch'. In truth, there's very little that won't be made better with a dusting of this magic mix of ingredients. While it's more common to find crispy fried foods paired with salt and chilli dishes, the seasoning itself can also be added to chow mein dishes to good effect.

SALT AND CHILLI CHICKEN

Crispy chicken, wok-fried vegetables and aromatic seasoning combine to create what is easily one of the most popular Chinese takeaway menu items. This is one of my absolute favourite things to order and to cook!

Serves 1

2 teaspoons vegetable oil
½ large onion, thinly sliced
¼ green pepper, deseeded and thinly sliced
½ carrot, thinly sliced
1 portion cooked Crispy Chicken (page 28)
2 teaspoons chopped Garlic in Oil (page 211)
1 green chilli, thinly sliced (optional)
1 generous teaspoon Salt and Pepper Seasoning (page 214), or to taste
1 spring onion, thinly sliced
½ teaspoon dried chilli flakes
1 teaspoon rice wine

- Heat a wok or large frying pan over a medium to high heat. Add the vegetable oil, sliced onion, green pepper and carrot and stir-fry for 1 minute.

- Add the crispy chicken pieces to the wok, then add the garlic in oil and green chilli (if using) and mix well. Add the salt and pepper seasoning and stir-fry for 30–40 seconds. Add the sliced spring onion and dried chilli flakes and mix well. Add the rice wine to finish, mix well once more and serve.

SALT AND CHILLI CHICKEN WINGS

Serves 1

2 teaspoons vegetable oil
½ large onion, thinly sliced
7 cooked Crispy Chicken Wings (page 52)
1 tablespoon chopped Garlic in Oil (page 211)
1 green chilli, thinly sliced (optional)
1 teaspoon Salt and Pepper Seasoning (page 214), or to
  taste
1 spring onion, thinly sliced
½ teaspoon dried chilli flakes
1 teaspoon rice wine

- Heat a wok or large frying pan over a medium to high heat. Add the vegetable oil and sliced onion and stir-fry for 1 minute.

- Add the crispy chicken wings, then add the garlic in oil and green chilli (if using) and mix well. Add the salt and pepper seasoning and stir-fry for 30–40 seconds. Add the sliced spring onion and dried chilli flakes and mix well, then add the rice wine to finish, mix well once more and serve.

SALT AND CHILLI KING PRAWNS

Serves 1

1 teaspoon vegetable oil
½ large onion, thinly sliced
1 portion cooked Crispy King Prawns (page 46)
2 teaspoons chopped Garlic in Oil (page 211)
1 generous teaspoon Salt and Pepper Seasoning (page 214), or to taste
1 spring onion, thinly sliced
½ teaspoon dried chilli flakes
1 teaspoon rice wine

- Heat a wok or large frying pan over a medium to high heat. Add the vegetable oil and sliced onion and stir-fry for 1 minute.

- Add the crispy king prawns and the garlic in oil and mix well. Add the salt and pepper seasoning and stir-fry for 30–40 seconds, then add the sliced spring onion and dried chilli flakes and mix well. Add the rice wine to finish, mix well once more and serve.

SALT AND CHILLI MINI SPRING ROLLS

This recipe is perfect when the salt and chilli cravings hit and need to be satisfied quickly; by using mini spring rolls you'll find in the freezer aisle of good Chinese supermarkets, the dish can be on the table in fifteen minutes!

Serves 1

Oil for deep-frying
9 mini vegetable spring rolls (I use Tsingtao brand)
1 teaspoon vegetable oil
½ large onion, thinly sliced
¼ green pepper, deseeded and thinly sliced
½ carrot, thinly sliced
2 teaspoons chopped Garlic in Oil (page 211)
1 generous teaspoon Salt and Pepper Seasoning (page 214), or to taste
1 spring onion, thinly sliced
½ teaspoon dried chilli flakes
1 teaspoon rice wine

- Heat the oil for deep-frying to 170°C/340°F. Add the mini spring rolls and fry for about 5 minutes, turning them occasionally with tongs, until the spring rolls are golden and crispy. Using a slotted spoon, remove the crispy mini spring rolls from the hot oil and set aside on a plate.

- Heat a wok or large frying pan over a medium to high heat. Add the teaspoon of vegetable oil, then add the sliced onion, green pepper and carrot and stir-fry for 1 minute.

- Add the fried mini spring rolls and the garlic in oil and mix well. Add the salt and pepper seasoning and stir-fry for 30–40 seconds, then add the sliced spring onion and dried chilli flakes and mix well. Add the rice wine to finish, mix well once more and serve.

SALT AND CHILLI CHIPS (IN LIGHT BATTER)

Serves 1–2

Oil for deep-frying
30g self-raising flour
Pinch of sea salt
Pinch of MSG
30ml cold water (you may need a little more)
250g frozen chips
1 tablespoon vegetable oil
½ large onion, thinly sliced
½ green pepper, deseeded and thinly sliced
½ carrot, thinly sliced
2 teaspoons chopped Garlic in Oil (page 211)
1 fresh green chilli, thinly sliced (optional)
1 teaspoon Salt and Pepper Seasoning (page 214), or to taste
1 spring onion, thinly sliced
½ teaspoon dried chilli flakes
1 teaspoon rice wine

- Heat the oil for deep-frying to 180°C/350°F.

- Put the self-raising flour, sea salt, MSG and water in a large bowl and mix well until a small amount of batter is formed (the batter should be a slightly thick paste). Add the frozen chips and mix thoroughly until each chip is lightly coated in the batter.

- Carefully add the battered chips to the hot oil, separating them as you go so that each chip hits the oil individually. Fry the chips for about 5 minutes until just beginning to colour, stirring occasionally. Using a slotted spoon, remove the chips from the hot oil and set aside on a plate. Increase the temperature of the oil to 190°C/375°F and return the battered chips to the oil. Fry for 2 minutes or until the chips are crispy and golden. Using a slotted spoon, remove the chips from the hot oil and set aside on a plate once again.

- Heat a wok or large frying pan over a medium to high heat. Add the tablespoon of vegetable oil, then add the sliced onion, green pepper and carrot and stir-fry for 1 minute.

- Add the battered chips and the garlic in oil and green chilli (if using) and mix well. Add the salt and pepper seasoning and stir-fry for 30–40 seconds. Add the sliced spring onion and dried chilli flakes and mix well. Add the rice wine to finish, mix well once more and serve.

SALT AND CHILLI HAGGIS BALLS

Serves 2 (makes 16 haggis balls)

On 25th January 2020, Chinese New Year and Burns Night in Scotland were celebrated simultaneously – I couldn't think of a better combination to pay tribute to both occasions than these delicious haggis bites, finished with traditional salt and chilli ingredients. You could, of course, use vegetarian haggis for this recipe if desired.

> 250g self-raising flour, plus 3 tablespoons for dusting the haggis slices
> ¼ teaspoon sea salt
> ¼ teaspoon MSG
> Pinch of ground white pepper
> 225–275ml cold water
> 4 haggis slices, quartered
> Oil for deep-frying
> 1 teaspoon vegetable oil
> 1 generous teaspoon Salt and Pepper Seasoning (page 214), or to taste
> 1 tablespoon rice wine

- Put the 250g self-raising flour, sea salt, MSG and white pepper in a large bowl, mix briefly and gradually add the water, whisking well until a thick batter is formed (you may not need all the water). Add more water if the batter is too thick, or more flour if the batter is too thin.

- Dust the haggis pieces with the 3 tablespoons of flour.

- Heat the oil for deep-frying to 170°C/340°F. Dip each piece of floured haggis in the batter until fully coated, drop carefully into the hot oil and fry for about 5 minutes or until the haggis balls are cooked through, crispy and golden. Remove from the oil using a slotted spoon, drain off any excess oil and set aside on a plate.

- Heat a wok or large frying pan over a medium to high heat. Add the teaspoon of vegetable oil, then add the fried haggis pieces to the pan and the salt and pepper seasoning, and stir-fry well for 30–40 seconds to coat the haggis balls evenly. Finish with the rice wine, transfer to a serving plate and serve.

SALT AND CHILLI PIZZA CRUNCH

Serves 1–2

'Deep-fry yer pizzas, we're gonnae deep-fry yer pizzas!' sang the tartan army of Scotland supporters during a football match against Italian opposition in recent years. It's funny because it's true: in Scotland, when it comes to tasty fast food, we're only too happy to take things up a notch. Chinese takeaway owners decided to take things further still by finishing battered pizza slices with traditional salt and chilli ingredients and a legendary dish was born.

250g self-raising flour
¼ teaspoon sea salt
¼ teaspoon MSG
Pinch of ground white pepper
225–275ml cold water
Oil for deep-frying
1 basic supermarket cheese pizza, quartered
1 teaspoon vegetable oil
½ large onion, thinly sliced
1 teaspoon chopped Garlic in Oil (page 211)
1 generous teaspoon Salt and Pepper Seasoning (page 214), or to taste
1 spring onion, thinly sliced
½ teaspoon dried chilli flakes
1 tablespoon rice wine

- Put the self-raising flour, sea salt, MSG and white pepper in a large bowl, mix briefly, then gradually add the water, whisking well until a thick batter is formed (you may not need all the water). The batter should be like a thick paste and should fall slowly off the back of a spoon. Add more water if the batter is too thick, or more flour if the batter is too thin.

- Heat the oil for deep-frying to 170°C/340°F. Dip each pizza slice in the batter until fully coated, then drop carefully cheese-side down into the hot oil and fry for about 1 minute until the batter is sealed and the underside is golden. Turn the pizza slices in the oil with tongs and fry for a further 1 minute or until cooked through, crispy and golden. Remove from the oil using a slotted spoon, drain off any excess oil and set aside on a plate.

- Heat a wok or large frying pan over a medium to high heat. Add the teaspoon of vegetable oil, then add the sliced onion and stir-fry for 30 seconds. Add the battered pizza slices, the chopped garlic and salt and pepper seasoning and stir-fry for 30–40 seconds. Add the spring onion and dried chilli flakes and mix once more. Finish with the rice wine, transfer to a serving plate and serve.

STIR-FRY DISHES

If you're a fan of Chinese takeaway food and frequent Chinese takeaway establishments, you'll be all too familiar with the immediately recognisable and enjoyable sound of sizzling stir-fry dishes being cooked in the restaurant kitchen. With intense heat and no shortage of flair, experienced takeaway chefs can easily take charge of several hot woks simultaneously, adding ingredients and stir-frying for just the right amount of time to ensure dishes are well fired and cooked to smoky perfection. Watching the chef in action, using a cooking range that offers intense heat, is a joy to behold and is an art and entertainment form all of its own.

We may not have access to the sort of high-heat burners that are available to restaurant chefs, but with the right ingredients and a good-quality carbon-steel wok, or even a regular non-stick wok, we can closely replicate some of those special stir-fry dishes we enjoy. While preparation is key in any form of cooking, it's perhaps more important in stir-fry cooking than any other. When it's time to cook, everything happens quickly – this means it's essential to have your ingredients prepared, marinated, chopped and close to hand to add to the hot wok immediately when called for.

This chapter includes recipes for a variety of stir-fry dishes – simply add your choice of cooked chicken, beef, char siu pork, king prawns, tofu or stir-fried vegetables as desired!

BROCCOLI AND OYSTER SAUCE STIR-FRY

Serves 1

1 tablespoon vegetable oil
½ large onion, thinly sliced
7–8 broccoli florets (about 75g)
1 portion cooked chicken, beef, char siu pork, king prawns
    or tofu (as desired)
¼ teaspoon MSG
1 teaspoon chopped Garlic in Oil (page 211)
200ml Light Chicken Stock (page 218), vegetable stock or
    water
1 tablespoon potato starch mixed with 2 tablespoons cold
    water
2 teaspoons rice wine

Sauce

2 tablespoons oyster sauce
1 teaspoon light soy sauce
1 teaspoon dark soy sauce
2 teaspoons tomato ketchup
Pinch of ground white pepper

- Put the sauce ingredients in a bowl, mix well and set aside.

- Heat a wok or large frying pan over a medium to high heat.
  Add the vegetable oil, then add the sliced onion and stir-fry

for 1 minute. Add the broccoli florets and stir-fry for a further 30–40 seconds, then add the cooked chicken, beef, char siu pork, king prawns or tofu.

- Add the MSG and chopped garlic in oil and mix well. Add the prepared sauce and mix well once more. Add the stock or water, bring to the boil and simmer for 2 minutes or until the sauce reduces slightly. Gradually add some of the starch-and-water mix, stirring well until the sauce reaches the desired consistency (you may not need all the mix). Add the rice wine, stir through and serve.

TOMATO STIR-FRY

Serves 1

1 tablespoon vegetable oil
½ large onion, roughly chopped
2 salad tomatoes, roughly chopped
1 portion cooked chicken, beef, char siu pork, king prawns
    or tofu (as desired)
Pinch of sea salt
Pinch of MSG
200ml Light Chicken Stock (page 218), vegetable stock or
    water
1 tablespoon potato starch mixed with 2 tablespoons cold
    water
1 spring onion, thinly sliced
2 teaspoons rice wine

Sauce

3 tablespoons tomato ketchup
1 teaspoon O.K. sauce
1 teaspoon light soy sauce
½ teaspoon dark soy sauce
1 tablespoon distilled clear malt vinegar
1 teaspoon caster sugar
1 teaspoon dark brown sugar

• Put the sauce ingredients in a bowl, mix well and set aside.

- Heat a wok or large frying pan over a medium to high heat. Add the vegetable oil, then add the chopped onion and stir-fry for 1 minute. Add the chopped tomatoes and stir-fry for a further 30–40 seconds, then add the cooked chicken, beef, char siu pork, king prawns or tofu.

- Add the sea salt and MSG and mix well. Add the prepared sauce and mix well once more. Add the stock or water, bring to the boil and simmer for 2 minutes or until the sauce reduces slightly. Gradually add some of the starch-and-water mix, stirring well until the sauce reaches the desired consistency (you may not need all the mix). Add the spring onion and mix well. Add the rice wine, stir through and serve.

BAMBOO SHOOT AND
WATER CHESTNUT STIR-FRY

Serves 1

1 tablespoon vegetable oil
¼ large onion, thinly sliced
¼ carrot, thinly sliced
1 handful tinned bamboo shoots, rinsed and drained
    (about 30g)
1 handful tinned water chestnuts, rinsed and drained
    (about 30g)
1 portion cooked chicken, beef, char siu pork, king prawns
    or tofu (as desired)
Pinch of sea salt
Pinch of MSG
1 generous teaspoon chopped Garlic in Oil (page 211)
125ml Light Chicken Stock (page 218), vegetable stock or
    water
1 tablespoon potato starch mixed with 2 tablespoons cold
    water
1 tablespoon rice wine
Dash of Aromatic Oil (page 212) or sesame oil
1 handful (about 30g) Toasted Cashew Nuts (see page 210)

Sauce

1 tablespoon oyster sauce
1 teaspoon light soy sauce

¼ teaspoon dark soy sauce
½ teaspoon tomato ketchup
Pinch of ground white pepper

- Put the sauce ingredients in a bowl, mix well and set aside.

- Heat a wok or large frying pan over a medium to high heat. Add the vegetable oil, then add the onion, carrot, bamboo shoots and water chestnuts and stir-fry for 1–2 minutes until the vegetables are lightly charred. Add the cooked chicken, beef, char siu pork, king prawns or tofu, then add the salt, MSG and chopped garlic in oil and mix well. Add the prepared sauce and mix well once more. Add the stock or water, bring to the boil and simmer for 1–2 minutes or until the sauce reduces slightly. Gradually add some of the starch-and-water mix, stirring well to thicken until the sauce reaches the desired consistency (you may not need all the mix). Add the rice wine and aromatic oil or sesame oil, stir through once more and serve topped with the toasted cashew nuts.

PINEAPPLE STIR·FRY

Serves 1

1 tablespoon vegetable oil
¼ large onion, sliced
¼ carrot, thinly sliced
5–6 tinned pineapple pieces
1 portion cooked chicken, beef, char siu pork, king prawns
 or tofu (as desired)
Pinch of sea salt
Pinch of MSG
125ml Light Chicken Stock (page 218), vegetable stock or
 water
1 tablespoon pineapple juice or syrup (from a tin)
1 tablespoon potato starch mixed with 2 tablespoons cold
 water
1–2 teaspoons rice wine

Sauce

1 tablespoon oyster sauce
1 teaspoon light soy sauce
¼ teaspoon dark soy sauce
½ teaspoon caster sugar
Pinch of ground white pepper

• Put the sauce ingredients in a bowl, mix well and set aside.

- Heat a wok or large frying pan over a medium to high heat. Add the vegetable oil, then add the onion, carrot and pineapple pieces and stir-fry for 1 minute. Add the cooked chicken, beef, char siu pork, king prawns or tofu, then add the salt and MSG and mix well. Add the prepared sauce and mix well once more. Add the stock or water, and pineapple juice or syrup, bring to the boil and simmer for 2 minutes or until the sauce reduces slightly. Gradually add some of the starch-and-water mix, stirring well until the sauce reaches the desired consistency (you may not need all the mix). Add the rice wine to taste, stir through and serve.

SWEETCORN AND STRAW MUSHROOM STIR-FRY

Serves 1

1 tablespoon vegetable oil
¼ large onion, thinly sliced
¼ carrot, thinly sliced
3 baby sweetcorn, roughly chopped
110g tinned straw mushrooms (about half a tin, rinsed and
    drained), halved
1 portion cooked chicken, beef, char siu pork, king prawns
    or tofu (as desired)
Pinch of sea salt
Pinch of MSG
1 generous teaspoon chopped Garlic in Oil (page 211)
125ml Light Chicken Stock (page 218), vegetable stock or
    water
1 tablespoon potato starch mixed with 2 tablespoons cold
    water
1 spring onion, thinly sliced
2 teaspoons rice wine

Sauce

1 tablespoon oyster sauce
1 teaspoon light soy sauce
¼ teaspoon dark soy sauce
1 teaspoon tomato ketchup
Pinch of ground white pepper

- Put the sauce ingredients in a bowl, mix well and set aside.

- Heat a wok or large frying pan over a medium to high heat. Add the vegetable oil, then add the onion, carrot, baby sweetcorn and straw mushrooms, mix well and stir-fry for 1–2 minutes until the vegetables are lightly charred. Add the cooked chicken, beef, char siu pork, king prawns or tofu, then add the salt, MSG and chopped garlic in oil and mix well. Add the prepared sauce and mix well once more. Add the stock or water, bring to the boil and simmer for 1–2 minutes or until the sauce reduces slightly. Gradually add some of the starch-and-water mix, stirring well until the sauce reaches the desired consistency (you may not need all the mix). Add the spring onion and mix well. Add the rice wine, stir through and serve.

MUSHROOM STIR-FRY

Full of umami flavour!

Serves 1

1 tablespoon vegetable oil
½ large onion, roughly chopped
6–8 button mushrooms, halved or quartered, depending on size
1 portion cooked chicken, beef, char siu pork, king prawns or tofu (as desired)
¼ teaspoon MSG
1 teaspoon chopped Garlic in Oil (page 211)
200ml Light Chicken Stock (page 218), vegetable stock or water
1 tablespoon potato starch mixed with 2 tablespoons cold water
2 teaspoons rice wine

Sauce

2 tablespoons oyster sauce
1 teaspoon light soy sauce
1 teaspoon dark soy sauce
2 teaspoons tomato ketchup
Pinch of ground white pepper

• Put the sauce ingredients in a bowl, mix well and set aside.

- Heat a wok or large frying pan over a medium to high heat. Add the vegetable oil, then add the sliced onion and mushrooms and stir-fry for 1–2 minutes until the vegetables are lightly charred. Add the cooked chicken, beef, char siu pork, king prawns or tofu, then add the MSG and chopped garlic in oil and mix well. Add the prepared sauce and mix well once more. Add the stock or water, bring to the boil and simmer for 2 minutes or until the sauce reduces slightly. Gradually add some of the starch-and-water mix, stirring well until the sauce reaches the desired consistency (you may not need all the mix). Add the rice wine, stir through and serve.

GINGER AND SPRING ONION STIR-FRY

Serves 1

1 tablespoon vegetable oil

2 garlic cloves, finely chopped

2.5cm piece of ginger, finely chopped

½ large onion, thinly sliced

2 spring onions, thinly sliced

1 portion cooked chicken, beef, char siu pork, king prawns or tofu (as desired)

¼ teaspoon sea salt

¼ teaspoon MSG

125ml Light Chicken Stock (page 218), vegetable stock or water

1 tablespoon potato starch mixed with 2 tablespoons cold water

1 tablespoon rice wine

Dash of Aromatic Oil (page 212) or sesame oil to finish (optional)

Sauce

1 tablespoon oyster sauce

½ teaspoon light soy sauce

½ teaspoon dark soy sauce

¼ teaspoon caster sugar

Pinch of ground white pepper

- Put the sauce ingredients in a bowl, mix well and set aside.

- Heat a wok or large frying pan over a medium to high heat. Add the vegetable oil, then add the garlic and ginger, mix well and stir-fry for 20 seconds. Add the sliced onion and stir-fry for 1 minute, then add the spring onions and stir-fry for a further 20 seconds. Add the cooked chicken, beef, char siu pork, king prawns or tofu, then add the salt and MSG and mix well. Add the prepared sauce and mix well once more. Add the stock or water, bring to the boil and simmer for 2 minutes or until the sauce reduces slightly. Gradually add some of the starch-and-water mix, stirring well until the sauce reaches the desired consistency (you may not need all the mix). Add the rice wine and aromatic oil or sesame oil, stir through and serve.

CHOP SUEY STIR-FRY

Serves 1

1 tablespoon vegetable oil

¼ large onion, thinly sliced

2 button mushrooms, halved or quartered depending on
size

¼ carrot, thinly sliced

1 small handful tinned bamboo shoots, rinsed and drained
(about 25g)

1 small handful tinned water chestnuts, rinsed and
drained (about 25g)

1 small handful beansprouts (about 50g)

1 portion cooked chicken, beef, char siu pork, king prawns
or tofu (as desired)

¼ teaspoon MSG

1 teaspoon chopped Garlic in Oil (page 211)

200ml Light Chicken Stock (page 218), vegetable stock or
water

1 tablespoon potato starch mixed with 2 tablespoons cold
water

2 teaspoons rice wine

Sauce

2 tablespoons oyster sauce

1 teaspoon light soy sauce

1 teaspoon dark soy sauce

2 teaspoons tomato ketchup
Pinch of ground white pepper

- Put the sauce ingredients in a bowl, mix well and set aside.

- Heat a wok or large frying pan over a medium to high heat. Add the vegetable oil, then add the sliced onion, mushrooms, carrot, bamboo shoots and water chestnuts and stir-fry for 1–2 minutes until the vegetables are lightly charred. Add the beansprouts and stir-fry for 1 minute. Add the cooked chicken, beef, char siu pork, king prawns or tofu, then add the MSG and chopped garlic in oil and mix well. Add the prepared sauce and mix well once more. Add the stock or water, bring to the boil and simmer for 2 minutes or until the sauce reduces slightly. Gradually add some of the starch-and-water mix, stirring well until the sauce reaches the desired consistency (you may not need all the mix). Add the rice wine, stir through and serve.

BLACK BEAN AND GREEN PEPPER STIR-FRY

Serves 1

1 tablespoon vegetable oil
½ large onion, roughly chopped
½ green pepper, deseeded and roughly chopped
¼ teaspoon sea salt
¼ teaspoon MSG
Pinch of ground white pepper
1 teaspoon dark soy sauce
175ml Light Chicken Stock (page 218), vegetable stock or
    water
1 portion cooked chicken, beef, char siu pork, king prawns
    or tofu (as desired)
1 teaspoon oyster sauce
1 tablespoon potato starch mixed with 2 tablespoons cold water
1 tablespoon rice wine

Black beans
20g fermented black beans
100ml hot water
2 teaspoons chopped Garlic in Oil (page 211)
¼ teaspoon caster sugar
Dash of sesame oil

• Put the black beans in a heatproof bowl, cover with the hot
  water and mix briefly. Set aside for 3 minutes, then rinse

and drain well and return the beans to the bowl. Add the chopped garlic in oil, caster sugar and sesame oil to the bowl and mix well, mashing some of the beans a little. Set aside in the fridge until needed (the mixture will keep well for up to 2 days).

- Heat a wok or large frying pan over a medium to high heat. Add the vegetable oil, then add the chopped onion and green pepper and stir-fry for 1 minute. Add the prepared black bean mix and stir-fry for a further 1 minute until aromatic.

- Add the salt, MSG, white pepper, dark soy sauce and stock or water. Mix well. Add the cooked chicken, beef, char siu pork, king prawns or tofu, mix well once more, bring the sauce to the boil and simmer for 2–3 minutes until the sauce reduces slightly.

- Add the oyster sauce and mix through. Thicken the sauce by gradually adding some of the starch-and-water mix until it reaches your desired consistency (you may not need all the mix). Finish the stir-fry with the rice wine and serve.

BLACK PEPPER STIR-FRY

A spicy and savoury dish.

Serves 1

1 tablespoon vegetable oil
½ large onion, roughly chopped
¼ red pepper, deseeded and roughly chopped
¼ green pepper, deseeded and roughly chopped
1 portion cooked chicken, beef, char siu pork, king prawns
  or tofu (as desired)
Pinch of sea salt
¼ teaspoon MSG
2 teaspoons chopped Garlic in Oil (page 211)
200ml Light Chicken Stock (page 218), vegetable stock or
  water
1 tablespoon potato starch mixed with 2 tablespoons cold water
1 spring onion, thinly sliced
2 teaspoons rice wine

Sauce
2 tablespoons oyster sauce
1 teaspoon light soy sauce
1 teaspoon dark soy sauce
¾ teaspoon ground black pepper
Pinch of ground white pepper
¼ teaspoon caster sugar

- Put the sauce ingredients in a bowl, mix well and set aside.

- Heat a wok or large frying pan over a medium to high heat. Add the vegetable oil, then add the chopped onion, red pepper and green pepper and stir-fry for 1–2 minutes. Add the cooked chicken, beef, char siu pork, king prawns or tofu, then add the salt, MSG and chopped garlic in oil and mix well. Add the prepared sauce and mix well once more. Add the stock or water, bring to the boil and simmer for 2 minutes or until the sauce reduces slightly. Gradually add some of the starch-and-water mix, stirring well until the sauce reaches the desired consistency (you may not need all the mix). Add the spring onion and mix well. Add the rice wine, stir through once more and serve.

SZECHUAN-STYLE STIR-FRY

Serves 1

1 tablespoon vegetable oil
¼ large onion, roughly chopped
¼ green pepper, deseeded and roughly chopped
¼ carrot, thinly sliced
1 handful tinned bamboo shoots, rinsed and drained
    (about 30g)
1 handful tinned water chestnuts, rinsed and drained
    (about 30g)
1 portion cooked chicken, beef, char siu pork, king prawns
    or tofu (as desired)
¼ teaspoon sea salt
¼ teaspoon MSG
1 tablespoon chopped Garlic in Oil (page 211)
¼ teaspoon dried chilli flakes
200ml Light Chicken Stock (page 218), vegetable stock or
    water
1 tablespoon potato starch mixed with 2 tablespoons cold water
1 spring onion, thinly sliced
1 tablespoon rice wine
1 fresh red chilli, sliced (optional), to serve

Sauce

1½ tablespoons hot bean sauce
1½ tablespoons tomato ketchup

1 teaspoon oyster sauce
1 teaspoon light soy sauce
¼ teaspoon dark soy sauce
1 teaspoon hoisin sauce
¼ teaspoon caster sugar
Pinch of white pepper

- Put the sauce ingredients in a bowl, mix well and set aside.

- Heat a wok or large frying pan over a medium to high heat. Add the vegetable oil, then add the chopped onion, green pepper, carrot, bamboo shoots and water chestnuts and stir-fry for 1–2 minutes. Add the cooked chicken, beef, char siu pork, king prawns or tofu, then add the salt, MSG, chopped garlic in oil and dried chilli flakes and mix well. Add the prepared sauce and mix well once more. Add the stock or water, bring to the boil and simmer for 2 minutes or until the sauce reduces slightly. Gradually add some of the starch-and-water mix, stirring well until the sauce reaches the desired consistency (you may not need all the mix). Add the spring onion and mix well. Add the rice wine and stir through once more. Garnish with fresh chilli, if using, and serve.

KUNG PO

Spicy, sweet and sour with cashew nuts.

Serves 1

1 tablespoon vegetable oil

¼ large onion, roughly chopped

¼ red pepper, deseeded and roughly chopped

¼ green pepper, deseeded and roughly chopped

1 small handful tinned bamboo shoots, rinsed and drained (about 25g)

1 small handful tinned water chestnuts, rinsed and drained (about 25g)

1 portion cooked chicken, beef, char siu pork, king prawns or tofu (as desired)

Pinch of ground white pepper

¼ teaspoon MSG

1 tablespoon hot bean sauce

1 tablespoon chopped Garlic in Oil (page 211)

¼ teaspoon dark soy sauce

1 tablespoon potato starch mixed with 2 tablespoons cold water

2 teaspoons rice wine

1 small handful Toasted Cashew Nuts (about 25g) (page 210), to serve

Sauce

   200ml water

   3 tablespoons caster sugar

   1½ tablespoons dark brown sugar

   20ml distilled clear malt vinegar

   ¼ teaspoon beetroot powder mixed with 1 tablespoon
      water

- First, make the sauce. Put the water in a saucepan, bring to the boil, then reduce the heat to medium-low. Add the caster sugar and dark brown sugar, mix well and simmer for 3 minutes. Add the vinegar and beetroot powder mixed with water, stir well and set aside.

- Heat a wok or large frying pan over a medium to high heat. Add the vegetable oil, then add the chopped onion, red pepper, green pepper, bamboo shoots and water chestnuts and stir-fry for 1–2 minutes. Add the cooked chicken, beef, char siu pork, king prawns or tofu, then add the white pepper and MSG and mix well. Add the hot bean sauce and chopped garlic in oil and stir-fry for 30 seconds. Add the dark soy sauce and prepared sauce and mix well once more. Bring to the boil and simmer for 2 minutes or until the sauce reduces slightly. Gradually add some of the starch-and-water mix, stirring well until the sauce reaches the desired consistency (you may not need all the mix). Add the rice wine to finish. Transfer the kung po to a serving plate, top with the toasted cashew nuts and serve.

SATAY STIR-FRY

Serves 1

1 generous tablespoon vegetable oil
¼ large onion, roughly chopped
¼ green pepper, roughly chopped
¼ red pepper, roughly chopped
¼ carrot, thinly sliced
1 portion cooked chicken, beef, char siu pork, king prawns
    or tofu (as desired)
1 generous teaspoon caster sugar
¼ teaspoon MSG
1 generous tablespoon chopped Garlic in Oil (page 211)
200ml Light Chicken Stock (page 218), vegetable stock or
    water
2 teaspoons Jimmy's saté sauce (or to taste)
1 tablespoon potato starch mixed with 2 tablespoons cold
    water
1 tablespoon rice wine

Sauce

2 tablespoons oyster sauce
1 teaspoon light soy sauce
½ teaspoon dark soy sauce

• Put the sauce ingredients in a bowl, mix well and set aside.

- Heat a wok or large frying pan over a medium to high heat. Add the vegetable oil, then add the chopped onion, green pepper, red pepper and carrot and stir-fry for 1 minute. Add the cooked chicken, beef, char siu pork, king prawns or tofu, then add the caster sugar, MSG and chopped garlic in oil and mix well. Add the prepared sauce and mix well once more. Add the stock or water, bring to the boil and simmer for 2 minutes or until the sauce reduces slightly. Add the saté sauce and mix well. Gradually add some of the starch-and-water mix, stirring well until the sauce reaches the desired consistency (you may not need all the mix). Add the rice wine, stir through and serve.

MONGOLIAN STIR-FRY

Serves 1

1 tablespoon vegetable oil

¼ large onion, thinly sliced

¼ red pepper, deseeded and thinly sliced

¼ green pepper, deseeded and thinly sliced

¼ carrot, thinly sliced

1 portion cooked chicken, beef, char siu pork, king prawns or tofu (as desired)

Pinch of sea salt

¼ teaspoon MSG

1 tablespoon chopped Garlic in Oil (page 211)

¼ teaspoon dried chilli flakes

200ml Light Chicken Stock (page 218), vegetable stock or water

1 tablespoon potato starch mixed with 2 tablespoons cold water

1 spring onion, thinly sliced

1 tablespoon rice wine

1 fresh green chilli, thinly sliced (optional), to serve

Sauce

2 tablespoons oyster sauce

1 teaspoon light soy sauce

1 teaspoon dark soy sauce

1 teaspoon hoisin sauce

¼ teaspoon sriracha sauce
Pinch of ground white pepper

- Put the sauce ingredients in a bowl, mix well and set aside.

- Heat a wok or large frying pan over a medium to high heat. Add the vegetable oil, then add the sliced onion, red pepper, green pepper and carrot and stir-fry for 1–2 minutes until the vegetables are lightly charred. Add the cooked chicken, beef, char siu pork, king prawns or tofu, then add the sea salt, MSG, chopped garlic in oil and dried chilli flakes and mix well. Add the prepared sauce and mix well once more. Add the stock or water, bring to the boil and simmer for 2 minutes or until the sauce reduces slightly. Gradually add some of the starch-and-water mix, stirring well until the sauce reaches the desired consistency (you may not need all the mix). Add the spring onion and mix well. Add the rice wine and stir through. Garnish with green chilli (if using) and serve.

CHILLI GARLIC STIR-FRY

A sweet and spicy dish, packed full of flavour.

Serves 1

1 tablespoon vegetable oil
¼ large onion, thinly sliced
¼ green pepper, deseeded and thinly sliced
¼ red pepper, deseeded and thinly sliced
¼ carrot, thinly sliced
1 portion cooked chicken, beef, char siu pork, king prawns
   or tofu (as desired)
Pinch of ground white pepper
¼ teaspoon MSG
1 tablespoon hot bean sauce
2 tablespoons chopped Garlic in Oil (page 211)
¼ teaspoon dark soy sauce
1 tablespoon potato starch mixed with 2 tablespoons cold
   water
1 spring onion, thinly sliced
1 tablespoon rice wine
1 fresh red chilli pepper, thinly sliced (optional)

Sauce
200ml water
3 tablespoons caster sugar
1 tablespoon soft dark brown sugar

10ml distilled clear white malt vinegar
¼ teaspoon beetroot powder mixed with 1 tablespoon
  water

- First, make the sauce. Bring the water to the boil in a saucepan, then reduce the heat to low to medium. Add the caster sugar and dark brown sugar, mix well and simmer for 3 minutes. Add the vinegar and beetroot powder mixed with water, stir well and set aside.

- Heat a wok or large frying pan over a medium to high heat. Add the vegetable oil, then add the sliced onion, green pepper, red pepper and carrot and stir-fry for 1–2 minutes. Add the cooked chicken, beef, char siu pork, king prawns or tofu, then add the white pepper, MSG and hot bean sauce and mix well. Add the chopped garlic in oil, the dark soy sauce and the prepared sauce and mix well once more. Bring to the boil and simmer for 2 minutes or until the sauce reduces slightly. Gradually add some of the starch-and-water mix, stirring well until the sauce reaches the desired consistency (you may not need all the mix). Add the spring onion and rice wine and mix well once more. Transfer the chilli garlic to a serving plate, top with the sliced fresh red chilli (if using) and serve.

CHEF'S SPECIALS

On many takeaway or restaurant menus you'll find a selection of 'Chef's Special' items – dishes the chef is most proud of and eager for hungry customers to try. Included in this chapter are some of my own favourite dishes, which I hope you'll find very special indeed.

CANTONESE-STYLE SWEET AND SOUR CHICKEN

A Chinese takeaway classic, my take on this recipe uses natural beetroot powder to provide the familiar bright pink colour to the finished sauce.

Serves 1

¼ large onion, roughly chopped
¼ red or yellow pepper, deseeded and roughly chopped
5–6 pineapple pieces (from a tin), to taste
1 tablespoon potato starch mixed with 2 tablespoons cold water
1 portion cooked Crispy Chicken (page 28)

Sauce
100ml water
50ml pineapple juice or syrup (from a tin)
3 tablespoons caster sugar
1 tablespoon dark brown sugar
20ml distilled clear malt vinegar
¼ teaspoon beetroot powder mixed with 1 tablespoon water

- First, make the sauce. Put the water and pineapple juice or syrup in a saucepan and bring to the boil. When the mix is boiling, add the white and brown sugar and mix well. Reduce the heat to low and simmer for 3 minutes. Add the vinegar and mix well. Add the beetroot-powder-and-water mix, stir well and set aside.

- Heat a wok or large frying pan over a medium to high heat. Add the prepared sweet and sour sauce and bring it back to the boil. Add the chopped onion, red or yellow pepper and pineapple pieces and mix well. Simmer for 1 minute.

- Thicken the sauce with the starch-and-water mix, adding it gradually until the sauce is slightly thickened (you may not need all the mix). Add the crispy chicken pieces to the sweet and sour sauce, mix well and serve.

LEMON CHICKEN

Serves 1

Lemon Sauce
   75ml double-strength lemon squash (no added sugar)
   1½ teaspoons fresh lemon juice or lemon dressing
   100ml water
   1 tablespoon caster sugar
   1 tablespoon golden syrup
   1 tablespoon potato starch mixed with 2 tablespoons cold
      water

Batter
   4 tablespoons potato starch
   1 tablespoon custard powder (original, not instant)
   ¼ teaspoon sea salt

Chicken
   1 skinless, boneless chicken breast fillet (about 150g)
   ¼ teaspoon sea salt
   ¼ teaspoon MSG
   Pinch of ground white pepper
   1 teaspoon rice wine
   1 egg
   Oil for deep-frying

- Put the lemon squash, fresh lemon juice or lemon dressing
  and water in a saucepan and bring to the boil. Add the

caster sugar and golden syrup, mix well, reduce the heat to low and simmer for 3 minutes. Increase the heat to medium to high and gradually add the starch-and-water mix, stirring well until the sauce reaches the desired consistency, bearing in mind that you may not need all the mix (the sauce should be a slightly thick glaze). Set aside.

- Put the batter ingredients – the potato starch, custard powder and sea salt – in a shallow bowl and mix well.

- Place the chicken breast fillet between two sheets of cling film and use a meat hammer or heavy rolling pin to pound the meat flat. Put the chicken breast on a large plate, sprinkle with the sea salt, MSG, white pepper and rice wine and press the seasoning into the chicken. Whisk the egg in a bowl and add just enough of the whisked egg as is needed to coat the chicken (about half the egg) – this helps the flour-and-custard-powder mix stick to the chicken.

- Heat oil for deep-frying to 180°C/350°F. Add the seasoned chicken to the prepared bowl of potato starch and custard powder and press down well to ensure the chicken breast is fully coated. Carefully place into the hot oil and fry for 5–6 minutes, turning it occasionally with tongs until the chicken is cooked through, golden and crispy. Remove the crispy chicken from the oil using tongs, drain off any excess oil on a plate lined with kitchen paper and place the crispy chicken on a plate.

- Cut the chicken into strips, top generously with the prepared lemon sauce and serve.

HOT AND SPICY CHICKEN SLICE

Serves 1

Batter
    3 tablespoons potato starch
    3 tablespoons custard powder (original, not instant)

Chicken
    1 skinless, boneless chicken breast fillet (about 150g)
    ¼ teaspoon sea salt
    ¼ teaspoon MSG
    Pinch of ground white pepper
    1 teaspoon rice wine
    1 egg
    Oil for deep-frying

Stir-fried hot and spicy vegetables
    1 tablespoon vegetable oil
    ½ onion, thinly sliced
    ½ green pepper, deseeded and thinly sliced
    1 generous tablespoon chopped Garlic in Oil (page 211)
    1 teaspoon Salt and Pepper Seasoning (page 214), or to taste
    1 spring onion, thinly sliced
    ½ teaspoon dried chilli flakes
    1 tablespoon rice wine

- Combine the potato starch and custard powder in a shallow bowl and set aside.

- Place the chicken breast fillet between two sheets of cling film and use a meat hammer or heavy rolling pin to pound the meat flat. Put the chicken breast on a large plate, sprinkle with the sea salt, MSG, white pepper and rice wine and press the seasoning into the chicken. Whisk the egg in a bowl and add just enough of the whisked egg as is needed to coat the chicken (about half the egg) – this helps the flour-and-custard-powder mix stick to the chicken.

- Heat oil for deep-frying to 180°C/350°F. Add the seasoned chicken to the prepared bowl of potato starch and custard powder and press down well to ensure the chicken breast is fully coated. Carefully place into the hot oil and fry for 5–6 minutes, turning it occasionally with tongs until the chicken is cooked through, golden and crispy. Remove the crispy chicken from the oil using tongs and drain off any excess oil on a plate lined with kitchen paper. Place the crispy chicken on a serving plate and cut the chicken into strips.

- For the vegetables, heat a wok or large frying pan over a medium to high heat. Add the vegetable oil, then add the sliced onion and green pepper and stir-fry for 30–40 seconds. Add the chopped garlic in oil, salt and pepper seasoning and spring onion and stir-fry for 30–40 seconds, then add the dried chilli flakes and mix well. Finish with the rice wine and serve on top of the crispy sliced chicken.

CHAR SIU PORK CRISPY NOODLES

Serves 1

1 portion Crispy Noodles (page 182)
1 tablespoon vegetable oil
1 portion cooked Char Siu Pork (page 36), about 125g,
    sliced
¼ large onion, thinly sliced
4 button mushrooms, halved
1 handful tinned bamboo shoots, rinsed and drained
    (about 30g)
1 handful tinned water chestnuts, rinsed and drained
    (about 30g)
1 small handful beansprouts (about 50g)
¼ teaspoon sea salt
¼ teaspoon MSG
1 teaspoon chopped Garlic in Oil (page 211)
175ml Light Chicken Stock (page 218), vegetable stock or
    water
1 tablespoon potato starch mixed with 2 tablespoons cold
    water
1 spring onion, thinly sliced
2 teaspoons rice wine

Sauce
2 teaspoons oyster sauce
2 teaspoons light soy sauce

¼ teaspoon dark soy sauce
¼ teaspoon caster sugar
Pinch of ground white pepper

- Put the sauce ingredients in a bowl, mix well and set aside.

- Prepare the crispy noodles and set aside.

- Heat a wok or large frying pan over a medium to high heat. Add the vegetable oil, then add the cooked pork, sliced onion, mushrooms, bamboo shoots and water chestnuts and stir-fry for 1 minute, then add the beansprouts and stir-fry for a further 30–40 seconds.

- Add the sea salt, MSG and chopped garlic in oil. Mix well. Add the prepared sauce and the stock or water, bring to the boil and simmer for 1–2 minutes or until the sauce is slightly reduced. Thicken the sauce by gradually adding the starch-and-water mix, stirring well until the sauce reaches the desired consistency (you may not need to use all the mix). Add the spring onion and mix once more. Finish with rice wine, pour on top of the crispy noodles and serve.

DAN DAN PORK NOODLES

This street-food-style noodle dish combines crispy pork mince with a hot bean sauce and fragrant coriander.

Serves 1

- 1 nest dried wheat noodles (about 210g) (I use the Lucky Boat brand)
- 1 tablespoon vegetable oil
- 125g pork mince
- 1 teaspoon chopped Garlic in Oil (page 211)
- 2 tablespoons water

Sauce

- 2 tablespoons hot bean sauce
- 2 tablespoons peanut butter
- 1 teaspoon light soy sauce
- 1 teaspoon dark soy sauce
- 1 teaspoon hoisin sauce
- 1 tablespoon rice wine
- Pinch of ground white pepper
- 50ml water

To serve

- 1 spring onion, thinly sliced
- 1 small handful fresh coriander, thinly sliced
- 1 teaspoon toasted white sesame seeds
- 1 tablespoon Chilli Oil (page 213)

- Put the sauce ingredients in a saucepan, mix and set aside.

- Put the dry noodle nest in a heatproof bowl and cover with boiling water. Let the noodles soak for about 3 minutes, using a chopstick to encourage them to separate as they soak. Drain and rinse the noodles in cold water to stop them from becoming too soft, drain well once again and set aside in a bowl.

- Heat a wok or large frying pan over a medium to high heat. Add the vegetable oil, then add the pork mince and stir-fry for 2–3 minutes or until the pork is browned. Add the chopped garlic in oil and stir-fry for a further 30 seconds, then add the water and fry the pork for another 3–4 minutes or until well cooked and crispy.

- Bring the prepared pan of sauce to the boil and simmer for 2–3 minutes until the sauce reduces and thickens slightly.

- Top the prepared bowl of noodles with the crispy pork and the simmering sauce. Garnish with sliced spring onion, fresh coriander and sesame seeds, drizzle with chilli oil, and serve.

CHINESE-STYLE CURRY

Serves 1

1 teaspoon vegetable oil
¼ onion, roughly chopped
225ml Light Chicken Stock (page 218), vegetable stock or
 water
¼ teaspoon sea salt
¼ teaspoon MSG
¼ teaspoon caster sugar
1 portion cooked chicken, beef, char siu pork, king
 prawns, tofu or mixed vegetables (as desired)
50g Chinese-style Curry Paste (page 215)

- Heat the vegetable oil in a saucepan over a high heat. Add
  the chopped onion and stir-fry for 30 seconds, then add the
  light chicken stock or water, sea salt, MSG and sugar. Mix
  well. Add the cooked chicken, beef, char siu pork, king
  prawns, tofu or mixed vegetables and mix well. Bring to the
  boil and simmer for 1 minute.

- Reduce the heat to low and add the curry paste. Mix well
  and simmer for a further 3–4 minutes, stirring often until
  the curry paste becomes smooth and begins to thicken,
  adding a little extra water if necessary, until the curry sauce
  reaches the desired consistency. Serve with Boiled Rice
  (page 161) or Egg Fried Rice (page 163).

SHREDDED AROMATIC PORK PANCAKES

Serves 4

This slow-cooked shredded pork combines perfectly with hoisin, fresh cucumber, spring onions and Chinese pancakes.

4 pork shoulder steaks (about 700g total weight)
1 teaspoon Salt and Pepper Seasoning (page 214), or to taste
1 tablespoon pork fat or sunflower oil
250ml Light Chicken Stock (page 218) or low-salt chicken stock from a cube
1 tablespoon hoisin sauce
1 whole star anise

To serve
24 Chinese pancakes (defrosted if frozen) (6 per person)
4 spring onions, thinly sliced
2 small cucumbers, deseeded and thinly sliced
Hoisin sauce

- Season the pork shoulder steaks with the salt and pepper seasoning and set aside for 5 minutes.

- Heat a large saucepan over a medium to high heat. Add the pork fat or sunflower oil, then add the pork shoulder steaks (working in batches if necessary) and fry for 1 minute on each side to brown. When all the pork steaks are browned, add the stock, hoisin sauce and star anise. Bring to the boil, cover, reduce the heat to low and simmer the pork for 1 hour 50 minutes.

- Remove the cooked pork from the stock and shred the meat with two forks. Mix it with 2–3 tablespoons of the remaining stock.

- Heat the Chinese pancakes according to the instructions (they can typically be either steamed for 5–6 minutes or microwaved for 20–30 seconds). Arrange the pancakes on serving plates and serve with the shredded pork, spring onions, cucumbers and hoisin sauce.

EUROPEAN-STYLE DISHES, OMELETTES AND FOO YUNG

Every chef and business owner hopes that their menu will include something for everyone, ensuring that a wide range of customers will be tempted by the delicious dishes on offer. To that end, and some may say as a way to satisfy 'fussy' customers who aren't sure about new tastes or experiences, many restaurants offer a European-style menu with retro favourites such as sirloin steak or omelette dishes, all, of course, accompanied by the ever-faithful portion of chips.

While at first glance these menu choices can seem boring or unexciting, your local takeaway chef knows what they're doing so these dishes are well worth trying. A Chinese omelette or foo yung dish is enough to satisfy the biggest of appetites!

SIRLOIN STEAK WITH ONION
AND MUSHROOM GRAVY

Serves 1

Onion and Mushroom Gravy
    2 tablespoons oyster sauce
    1 teaspoon light soy sauce
    1 teaspoon dark soy sauce
    2 teaspoons tomato ketchup
    Pinch of ground white pepper
    1 teaspoon vegetable oil
    ¼ large onion, thinly sliced
    3 button mushrooms, thinly sliced
    Pinch of sea salt
    Pinch of MSG
    1 teaspoon chopped Garlic in Oil (page 211)
    200ml Light Chicken Stock (page 218), vegetable stock or
        water
    1 tablespoon potato starch mixed with 2 tablespoons cold
        water
    1 tablespoon rice wine

Steak
    1 x 200g beef sirloin steak
    ¼ teaspoon sea salt
    ¼ teaspoon ground black pepper
    1 tablespoon vegetable oil

- Put the oyster sauce, light soy sauce, dark soy sauce, tomato ketchup and white pepper in a bowl, mix briefly and set aside.

- To make the gravy, heat the vegetable oil in a saucepan, add the sliced onion and mushrooms and stir-fry for 1–2 minutes until the vegetables are lightly charred. Add the salt, MSG and chopped garlic in oil and mix well, then add the prepared sauce, bring to the boil and simmer for 1–2 minutes or until the gravy is slightly reduced. Gradually thicken the gravy with some of the starch-and-water mix, stirring well until the gravy reaches the desired consistency (you may not need all the mix). Finish with the rice wine and leave over a low heat until needed, stirring occasionally.

- Heat a wok or large frying pan over a medium to high heat. Use a meat hammer or a heavy rolling pin to beat the steak thoroughly until thin (this will help to tenderise the steak). Add the sea salt, black pepper and vegetable oil and mix well, rubbing the mix into the steak until evenly seasoned. Add the seasoned steak to the wok or pan and press down gently to ensure even browning. Fry for about 1 minute, then turn the steak over and fry for a further 1–2 minutes or until just cooked through and well browned.

- Remove the steak from the pan and set aside to rest for 3 minutes. Transfer the sirloin steak to a serving plate, top generously with the onion and mushroom gravy and serve.

CHEESE OMELETTE

Serves 1

3 eggs
2 teaspoons cold water
¼ teaspoon sea salt
¼ teaspoon MSG
Dash of sesame oil
1 tablespoon vegetable oil
1 handful grated mild Cheddar cheese (or Cheddar and
    mozzarella mix)
Pinch of ground white pepper
Pinch of ground black pepper
1 salad tomato, halved, to serve

- Put the eggs, water, sea salt, MSG and sesame oil in a bowl, whisk thoroughly and set aside.

- Heat a wok or large frying pan over a medium heat. Add the vegetable oil.

- Whisk the eggs briefly once more then add them to the wok or pan, moving the pan in a circular motion to ensure the egg covers the base of the pan. Scatter the grated cheese around the middle of the egg in the pan and let the egg cook for 1–2 minutes, continuing to move the pan in a circular motion to encourage any uncooked egg to the edges of the pan. Increase the heat to high and the omelette should begin to move freely in the pan. Sprinkle the white pepper and black pepper over the omelette, then fold the omelette up from each side to cover the grated cheese in the middle. Flip the folded omelette in the pan and cook for a further 30 seconds. Slide the cheese omelette onto a plate and serve with fresh tomato.

MUSHROOM OMELETTE

Serves 1

3 eggs
2 teaspoons cold water
¼ teaspoon sea salt
¼ teaspoon MSG
Dash of sesame oil
1 tablespoon vegetable oil, plus extra if needed
3 button mushrooms, thinly sliced
Pinch of ground white pepper
Pinch of ground black pepper
1 salad tomato, halved, to serve

- Put the eggs, water, sea salt, MSG and sesame oil in a bowl, whisk thoroughly and set aside.

- Heat a wok or large frying pan over a medium to high heat. Add the vegetable oil, then add the sliced mushrooms and stir-fry for 1–2 minutes. Tip the cooked mushrooms onto a plate and set aside.

- Add a little more oil to the pan if necessary. Reduce the heat to medium, whisk the eggs briefly once more then add them to the wok or pan, moving the pan in a circular motion to ensure the egg covers the base of the pan. Scatter the cooked mushrooms around the middle of the egg in the pan and let the egg cook for 1–2 minutes, continuing to move the pan in a circular motion to encourage any uncooked egg to the edges of the pan. Increase the heat to high and the omelette should begin to move freely in the pan. In one quick (and skilful) motion, flip the omelette in the pan. Press down with a spatula to encourage the bottom of the omelette to brown a little, season with the white and black pepper and cook for a further 1 minute. Slide the mushroom omelette onto a plate and serve with fresh tomato.

ROAST PORK FOO YUNG

This dish is essentially a broken-up omelette, which is ideal if a Chinese-style omelette was your first idea but things went a little wrong during cooking.

Serves 1

3 eggs
2 teaspoons cold water
¼ teaspoon sea salt
¼ teaspoon MSG
Dash of sesame oil
1 tablespoon vegetable oil, plus extra if needed
¼ large onion, thinly sliced
1 small handful Char Siu Pork (page 36), about 75g, sliced
1 small handful beansprouts (about 50g)
Pinch of ground white pepper
Pinch of ground black pepper
1 spring onion, thinly sliced

- Put the eggs, water, sea salt, MSG and sesame oil in a bowl, whisk thoroughly and set aside.

- Heat a wok or large frying pan over a medium to high heat. Add the vegetable oil and tilt it around the pan, then add the sliced onion and char siu pork and stir-fry for

30–40 seconds, then add the beansprouts and stir-fry for a further 1 minute. Remove from the pan and set aside.

- Add a little more oil to the pan if necessary. Add the whisked egg mixture and swirl it around the pan. Let the egg begin to set for a few seconds, then gently stir-fry for 30–40 seconds, stirring and breaking up the egg into pieces as it sets. Add the cooked pork and vegetables, season with the white and black pepper and mix well. Add the spring onion, mix once more and serve.

RICE AND NOODLES

Despite its name on most menus, boiled rice cooked in a rice cooker is technically cooked by what's known as 'the absorption method'. Regardless, using a rice cooker to cook your rice ensures perfect results every time. For fried rice, cook the rice the day before, cool it down quickly, cover and set aside in the fridge overnight before use. This dries the rice out slightly and results in a fried rice dish which is much tastier than using freshly cooked rice, as well as being much easier to make (no wet rice sticking to the wok!).

Jasmine rice is fragrant, with a soft texture, whereas long-grain rice has a firmer texture but not as much flavour. My friend Chin Taylor, from Ziang's Kitchen, recommends using a combination of both jasmine rice and long-grain rice, and I've taken his advice on board with glee! Chin and his mum Choo have a large Internet presence and a lot of industry knowledge and information to share, so if you haven't already done so, it's well worth looking them up.

Noodles purchased in traditional supermarkets pale in comparison to those you'll find in Chinese supermarkets.

Don't be put off by the large quantities these noodles are sold in – they're a dried product and will live quite happily in your store cupboard for several months. As a general rule, paying attention to the brands and products sold in the biggest quantity in Chinese supermarkets is a great way to ensure you're using the same brands and ingredients your local takeaway chef might use. If it comes in 9kg boxes or 5-gallon bottles, it's probably used often!

BOILED RICE (RICE-COOKER METHOD)

Serves 1

1/3 rice-cooker cup of jasmine rice
2/3 rice-cooker cup of long-grain rice

- Put the jasmine rice and long-grain rice in a bowl and cover with fresh water. Mix the rice briefly by hand to agitate it – the water will become cloudy as excess starch is released from the rice. Drain the water and repeat the process twice more until the water is clear. Give the rice a final rinse with water, drain well and tip into the rice-cooker pot.

- Add water to the '1 cup' level indicated in your rice cooker. When the rice is cooked, fluff it up with a rice spoon, close the lid and leave on 'keep warm' setting for 10 minutes. The rice is now ready to serve.

- For fried rice: remove the rice from the pot and spread it out on a large plate. Set aside for 5 minutes. After 5 minutes, transfer the rice to a different plate, flipping the rice over as you do so (you'll see excess moisture left behind on the first plate). Fan the rice with the lid of a food container for 3–4 minutes until it's completely cooled down. Transfer the cooked and cooled rice to a lidded container and chill in the fridge overnight.

BOILED RICE (STOVETOP METHOD)

Serves 1

> 50g jasmine rice
> 100g long-grain rice
> 225ml cold water

- Put the jasmine rice and long-grain rice in a bowl and cover with fresh water. Mix the rice briefly by hand to agitate it – the water will become cloudy as excess starch is released from the rice. Drain the water and repeat the process twice more until the water is clear. Give the rice a final rinse with water, drain well and tip into a saucepan.

- Add the cold water. Bring to the boil over a high heat and, as soon as the water begins to boil, reduce the heat to the lowest available setting and cover the pan with a lid. Let the rice cook for 12 minutes. Remove from the heat and let the rice stand for another 10 minutes, resisting the urge to lift the lid. Fluff the rice up with a fork and it's ready to serve.

EGG-FRIED RICE (DRY DISH)

This recipe uses cooked and cooled rice which has been refrigerated overnight – if time is short and you haven't planned ahead, supermarket pouches of long-grain rice can be stir-fried (as described below) with reasonable results.

Serves 1

1 egg
1 teaspoon cold water
Dash of sesame oil
Pinch of ground white pepper
Pinch of ground black pepper
1 portion cooked rice, cooled and refrigerated overnight (page 161/162)
¼ teaspoon sea salt
¼ teaspoon MSG
1 teaspoon dark soy sauce
1 tablespoon vegetable oil

- Put the egg, water, sesame oil, white pepper and black pepper in a small bowl and whisk thoroughly.

- Put the cooked and cooled rice, sea salt, MSG and dark soy sauce in a large bowl. Mix well with a fork, breaking up any clumps of rice which have stuck together.

- Heat a wok or large frying pan over a medium heat. Add the vegetable oil, then add the prepared whisked egg mixture. Stir-fry the egg for 20 seconds until it's scrambled and almost cooked through. Add a little more oil to the pan if needed. Add the prepared rice, mix well and stir-fry for 2–3 minutes until the rice is piping hot.

- Increase the heat to high and continue to stir-fry the rice for a further minute or so until the texture is dry and the rice grains appear to pop or dance around in the middle of the wok. Transfer the egg-fried rice to a serving plate and serve alongside your favourite stir-fry dishes.

CHICKEN/PORK/BEEF/KING PRAWN
FRIED RICE (DRY DISH)

Serves 1

1 egg
Dash of sesame oil
1 portion cooked rice, cooled and refrigerated overnight
　　(page 161/162)
¼ teaspoon sea salt
¼ teaspoon MSG
1 teaspoon dark soy sauce
1 tablespoon vegetable oil
1 portion cooked chicken, beef, char siu pork, king prawns
　　or tofu (as desired)
Pinch of ground white pepper
Pinch of ground black pepper
1 teaspoon chopped Garlic in Oil (page 211)

- Put the egg and sesame oil in a small bowl and whisk thoroughly.

- Put the cooked and cooled rice, sea salt, MSG and dark soy sauce in a large bowl. Mix well with a fork, breaking up any clumps of rice which have stuck together.

- Heat a wok or large frying pan over a medium heat. Add the vegetable oil, then add the prepared whisked egg mixture. Stir-fry the egg for 20 seconds until it's scrambled and almost cooked through. Add the cooked chicken, beef, pork, king prawns or tofu and stir-fry for 30 seconds. Add the prepared rice, mix well and stir-fry for 2–3 minutes until the rice is piping hot.

- Increase the heat to high and continue to stir-fry the rice until the texture is dry and the rice grains appear to pop or dance around in the middle of the wok. Add the white pepper, black pepper and garlic in oil and stir-fry for 20 seconds. Transfer the chicken-fried rice to a plate and serve.

CHICKEN-FRIED RICE WITH SAUCE

Serves 1

1 portion cooked Egg-fried Rice (page 163)
1 tablespoon vegetable oil
1 portion cooked Chicken Thighs (page 26)
1 teaspoon chopped Garlic in Oil (page 211)
125ml Light Chicken Stock (page 218), vegetable stock or
    water
1 tablespoon potato starch mixed with 2 tablespoons cold
    water
1 spring onion, thinly sliced
1 teaspoon rice wine

Sauce
2 tablespoons oyster sauce
2 teaspoons light soy sauce
2 teaspoons dark soy sauce
2 teaspoons tomato ketchup
Pinch of ground white pepper

- Put the sauce ingredients in a bowl, mix well and set aside.

- Prepare the egg-fried rice and transfer the rice to a foil tray
  or food container. Cover to keep warm.

- Heat a wok or large frying pan over a medium to high heat.
  Add the vegetable oil and the cooked chicken and stir-fry

for 1 minute, then add the prepared sauce. Add the stock or water, bring to the boil and simmer for 1 minute or until the sauce reduces slightly. Gradually add some of the starch-and-water mix, stirring well until the sauce reaches the desired consistency (you may not need all the mix). Add the spring onion and the rice wine, mix well once more and pour the chicken and sauce over the prepared egg-fried rice.

SPECIAL FRIED RICE

Serves 1

1 egg
Dash of sesame oil
Pinch of ground white pepper
Pinch of ground black pepper
1 portion cooked rice, cooled and refrigerated overnight
    (page 161/162)
¼ teaspoon sea salt
¼ teaspoon MSG
1 teaspoon dark soy sauce
1 tablespoon vegetable oil
1 small handful each cooked chicken breast, char siu pork
    and king prawns
1 teaspoon chopped Garlic in Oil (page 211) (optional)

- Put the egg, sesame oil, white pepper and black pepper in a small bowl and whisk thoroughly.

- Put the cooked and cooled rice, sea salt, MSG and dark soy sauce in a large bowl. Mix well with a fork, breaking up any clumps of rice which have stuck together.

- Heat a wok or large frying pan over a medium heat. Add the vegetable oil, then the cooked chicken, char siu pork and king prawns. Stir-fry for 1 minute, then add the prepared whisked egg mixture. Stir-fry the egg for

169

20 seconds until it's scrambled and almost cooked through. Add the prepared rice, mix well and stir-fry for 2–3 minutes until the rice is piping hot.

- Increase the heat to high and continue to stir-fry the rice for another minute or so until the texture is dry and the rice grains appear to pop or dance around in the middle of the wok. Finish with the garlic in oil, if using, transfer the special fried rice to a serving plate and serve.

SINGAPORE-STYLE FRIED RICE

Serves 1

1 egg
Dash of sesame oil
Pinch of ground white pepper
Pinch of ground black pepper
1 portion cooked rice, cooled and refrigerated overnight
    (page 161/162)
¼ teaspoon sea salt
¼ teaspoon MSG
1 teaspoon dark soy sauce
1 tablespoon vegetable oil
1 small handful each cooked chicken breast, char siu pork
    and king prawns
1 teaspoon Chinese-style Curry Paste (page 215)

- Put the egg, sesame oil, white pepper and black pepper in
  a small bowl and whisk thoroughly.

- Put the cooked and cooled rice, sea salt, MSG and dark soy
  sauce in a large bowl. Mix well with a fork, breaking up any
  clumps of rice which have stuck together.

- Heat a wok or large frying pan over a medium heat. Add
  the vegetable oil, then the cooked chicken, char siu pork
  and king prawns. Stir-fry for 1 minute, then add the
  prepared whisked egg mixture. Stir-fry the egg for

20 seconds until it's scrambled and almost cooked through. Add the prepared rice, mix well and stir-fry for 2–3 minutes until the rice is piping hot. Add the curry paste and mix well through the rice.

- Increase the heat to high and continue to stir-fry the rice for another minute or so until the texture is dry and the rice grains appear to pop or dance around in the middle of the wok. Transfer the Singapore-fried rice on to a serving plate and serve.

PLAIN CHOW MEIN (SOFT NOODLES)

Serves 1

1 nest dried wheat noodles (about 210g) (I use the Lucky
  Boat brand)
1 tablespoon vegetable oil
¼ large onion, thinly sliced
1 handful beansprouts (about 100g)
1 tablespoon dark soy sauce
50ml water
1 teaspoon light soy sauce
¼ teaspoon sea salt
¼ teaspoon MSG
¼ teaspoon caster sugar
Pinch of ground white pepper
1 spring onion, thinly sliced
1 teaspoon Aromatic Oil (page 212) or sesame oil

- Put the dried noodle nest in a heatproof bowl and cover
  with boiling water. Let the noodles soak for about
  3 minutes, using a chopstick to encourage them to separate
  as they soak. Drain and rinse the noodles in cold water to
  stop them from becoming too soft, drain well once again
  and set aside.

- Heat a wok or large frying pan over a medium to high heat.
  Add the vegetable oil and swirl it well around the pan, add

the sliced onion, then place the beansprouts on top, followed by the prepared noodles. Add the dark soy sauce and water and let the ingredients fry untouched for 30–40 seconds.

- Add the light soy sauce, sea salt, MSG, sugar and white pepper. Stir-fry the noodles well for 1 minute. Add the sliced spring onion and mix through. Finish with the aromatic oil or sesame oil and serve.

CHOW MEIN

Serves 1

1 nest dried wheat noodles (about 210g) (I use the Lucky
   Boat brand)
1 tablespoon vegetable oil
1 portion cooked chicken, beef, char siu pork, king prawns
   or tofu (as desired)
¼ large onion, thinly sliced
1 handful beansprouts (about 100g)
1 tablespoon dark soy sauce
50ml water
1 teaspoon light soy sauce
¼ teaspoon sea salt
¼ teaspoon MSG
¼ teaspoon caster sugar
Pinch of ground white pepper
1 spring onion, thinly sliced
1 teaspoon Aromatic Oil (page 212) or sesame oil

- Put the dried noodle nest in a heatproof bowl and cover
  with boiling water. Let the noodles soak for about
  3 minutes, using a chopstick to encourage them to separate
  as they soak. Drain and rinse the noodles in cold water to
  stop them from becoming too soft, drain well once again
  and set aside.

- Heat a wok or large frying pan over a medium to high heat. Add the vegetable oil and swirl it well around the pan. Add the cooked chicken, beef, char siu pork, king prawns or tofu and stir-fry for 1 minute, then add the sliced onion. Place the beansprouts on top, followed by the prepared noodles. Add the dark soy sauce and water and let the ingredients fry untouched for 30–40 seconds.

- Add the light soy sauce, sea salt, MSG, sugar and white pepper. Stir-fry the noodles well for 1 minute. Add the sliced spring onion and mix through. Finish with the aromatic oil or sesame oil and serve.

CHICKEN CHOW MEIN WITH OYSTER SAUCE

Serves 1

Noodles

    1 nest dried wheat noodles (about 210g) (I use the Lucky
       Boat brand)

    1 tablespoon vegetable oil

    ¼ large onion, thinly sliced

    1 handful beansprouts (about 100g)

    1 teaspoon dark soy sauce

    50ml water

    ½ teaspoon light soy sauce

    ¼ teaspoon sea salt

    ¼ teaspoon MSG

    ¼ teaspoon caster sugar

    Pinch of ground white pepper

    1 spring onion, thinly sliced

    1 teaspoon Aromatic Oil (page 212) or sesame oil

Chicken and Sauce

    2 tablespoons oyster sauce

    1 teaspoon light soy sauce

    1 teaspoon dark soy sauce

    2 teaspoons tomato ketchup

    Pinch of ground white pepper

    2 teaspoons vegetable oil

    1 portion Cooked Chicken Thighs (page 26), sliced

125ml Light Chicken Stock (page 218) or water

1 tablespoon potato starch mixed with 2 tablespoons cold
water

1 tablespoon rice wine

- First, prepare the noodles. Put the dried noodle nest in a heatproof bowl and cover with boiling water. Let the noodles soak for about 3 minutes, using a chopstick to encourage them to separate as they soak. Drain and rinse the noodles in cold water to stop them from becoming too soft, drain well once again and set aside.

- Heat a wok or large frying pan over a medium to high heat. Add the vegetable oil and swirl it well around the pan, add the sliced onion, then place the beansprouts on top, followed by the prepared noodles. Add the dark soy sauce and water and let the ingredients fry untouched for 30–40 seconds.

- Add the light soy sauce, sea salt, MSG, sugar and white pepper. Stir-fry the noodles well for 1 minute. Add the sliced spring onion and mix through. Finish with the aromatic oil or sesame oil, set the noodles aside on a serving plate and wipe the wok or frying pan clean.

- To make the sauce, put the oyster sauce, light soy sauce, dark soy sauce, tomato ketchup and white pepper in a bowl, mix well and set aside.

- Heat the wok or large frying pan over a medium to high heat. Add the 2 teaspoons of vegetable oil, then add the cooked chicken thighs and stir-fry for 2 minutes or until the chicken is piping hot. Add the prepared sauce and mix well. Add the stock or water, bring to the boil and simmer for 2 minutes or until the sauce is slightly reduced. Gradually add some of the starch-and-water mix, stirring well until the sauce has reached the desired consistency (you may not need all the mix).

- Add the rice wine and mix well once more. Ladle the sizzling chicken and sauce over the prepared chow mein and serve.

SALT AND CHILLI CHOW MEIN

Serves 1

1 nest dried wheat noodles (about 210g) (I use the Lucky Boat brand)

1 tablespoon vegetable oil

1 portion cooked chicken, beef, char siu pork, king prawns or tofu (as desired)

¼ large onion, thinly sliced

¼ green pepper, deseeded and thinly sliced

¼ red pepper, deseeded and thinly sliced

1 handful beansprouts (about 100g)

1 tablespoon dark soy sauce

50ml water

½ teaspoon light soy sauce

1 teaspoon Salt and Pepper Seasoning (page 214), or to taste

1 spring onion, thinly sliced

1 teaspoon chopped Garlic in Oil (page 211)

1 teaspoon rice wine

1 fresh red chilli, thinly sliced

- First, prepare the noodles. Put the dried noodle nest in a heatproof bowl and cover with boiling water. Let the noodles soak for about 3 minutes, using a chopstick to encourage them to separate as they soak. Drain and rinse the noodles in cold water to stop them from becoming too soft, drain well once again and set aside.

- Heat a wok or large frying pan over a medium to high heat. Add the vegetable oil and swirl it well around the pan, add the cooked chicken, beef, char siu pork or king prawns and stir-fry for 1 minute. Add the sliced onion, green pepper and red pepper, then place the beansprouts on top, followed by the prepared noodles. Add the dark soy sauce and water and let the ingredients fry untouched for 30–40 seconds.

- Add the light soy sauce and salt and pepper seasoning. Stir-fry the noodles well for 1 minute. Add the sliced spring onion and chopped garlic in oil and mix through. Finish with the rice wine, mix well once more and pour the chow mein onto a serving plate. Garnish with sliced red chilli (if using) and serve.

CRISPY NOODLES

This crispy noodle base can be topped with any of your favourite stir-fries to create a crispy chow mein dish.

Serves 1

1 nest dried wheat noodles (about 210g) (I use the Lucky Boat brand)
1 tablespoon vegetable oil

- Put the dried noodle nest in a heatproof bowl and cover with boiling water. Let the noodles soak for about 3 minutes, using a chopstick to encourage them to separate as they soak. Drain and rinse the noodles in cold water to stop them from becoming too soft, drain well once again and set aside.

- Heat a wok or non-stick frying pan over a medium heat. Add the vegetable oil and swirl it around the pan until evenly coated. Add the noodles and spread them out around the pan. Fry the noodles for 3–4 minutes, flip and continue to cook for a further 3 minutes on the other side, or until the noodles are crispy. Keep an eye on the heat as the noodles cook – the aim is to toast the noodles until they dry out and become crisp.

- Transfer the noodles to a serving plate and top with your favourite stir-fry dishes.

SINGAPORE VERMICELLI NOODLES

Serves 1

1 teaspoon light soy sauce

½ teaspoon dark soy sauce

¼ teaspoon caster sugar

½ teaspoon chopped Garlic in Oil (page 211)

1 teaspoon water

200g vermicelli rice noodles

1 tablespoon vegetable oil

¼ large onion, thinly sliced

½ small carrot, thinly sliced

Pinch of sea salt

Pinch of MSG

Pinch of ground white pepper

1 fresh red chilli, thinly sliced

1 small handful beansprouts (about 50g)

1 egg, beaten

1 small handful each cooked chicken, beef, char siu pork
and king prawns

1 tablespoon Chinese-style Curry Paste (page 215)

1 spring onion, thinly sliced

- Put the light soy sauce, dark soy sauce, sugar, chopped garlic in oil and water in a bowl, mix briefly and set aside.

- Put the vermicelli rice noodles in a heatproof bowl and cover with boiling water. Let the noodles soak for about 3 minutes, using a chopstick to encourage them to separate as they soak. Drain and rinse the noodles briefly in cold water, drain again and set aside.

- Heat a wok or large frying pan over a medium to high heat. Add the vegetable oil, then add the sliced onion and carrot and stir-fry for 30–40 seconds. Add the salt, MSG and white pepper and mix well, then add the sliced red chilli and beansprouts and stir-fry for a further 30 seconds.

- Push the ingredients in the pan to one side and add the egg to the pan. Stir-fry for 30 seconds. Add the cooked chicken, beef, char siu pork and king prawns and mix well, then add the prepared noodles and sauce and stir-fry for 1 minute. Add the curry paste and stir-fry for 1–2 more minutes, until the noodles and vegetables are evenly coated. Add the spring onion, mix well once more and serve.

SIDE DISHES

When I'm putting together an order from my local Chinese takeaway, no matter what starters and main courses I choose, I won't be dissuaded in any way from adding extra sides, particularly if eating with friends. Crispy chips and prawn crackers are the ideal vessel for any leftover stir-fry or curry sauces, while stir-fried vegetables such as beansprouts or broccoli help to accompany the more indulgent dishes.

This chapter includes recipes for some of the most popular side dishes you'll find on takeaway menus. Remember, you can mix and match the recipes in this book to good effect based on your own preferences – salt and chilli French-fried onion rings, anyone?

CHIPS

Chinese takeaways and restaurants commonly use frozen precooked chips and fry them in oil which has been used to cook various aromatic and tasty items such as crispy chicken, spring rolls, spare ribs and more. This adds a unique flavour to takeaway chips and is tricky to replicate at home.

In order to best replicate takeaway chips, first try to obtain frozen chips from your local Chinese supermarket. Brands such as Lamb Weston, Aviko and Farm Frites are all commonly used chips that you can look out for. If you like, you can fry your chips in some oil you've previously used to cook some of the other dishes in this book. When using frozen precooked chips purchased from Chinese supermarkets, I've had good results using an air fryer to cook the chips, so it's well worth giving this a try if you have one.

See Salt and Chilli Chips (in a light batter) (page 96)

HOMEMADE CHIPS

My good friend Louise Boyle recently moved from Scotland to Thailand and I've often found myself green with envy at the wide range of tasty dishes she has available to her. One thing I know she misses from her time in Scotland however is 'real' chips, so this recipe is for her, and for you, if you'd like to cook your chips from scratch.

Serves 1–2

2 large floury potatoes (Maris Piper or King Edward are ideal)
Oil for deep-frying

- Cut the potatoes into chunky chips (you can leave the skin on if you prefer) – aim for a chip which is slightly larger than the size you'd like to finish with, as the chipped potatoes will reduce in size during cooking.

- Tip the chipped potatoes into a large bowl and cover with fresh water. Stir well to agitate – the water will become cloudy as the potato releases its starch. Drain the chipped potatoes, rinse well again and drain once more. Pat dry with kitchen paper – the drier you can get your potatoes at this stage, the better they'll crisp up during cooking.

- Heat oil for deep-frying to about 160°C/320°F. Carefully add the chipped potatoes to the hot oil and fry for

4–5 minutes, until the chips just begin to soften and colour slightly. Remove the chips from the oil with a slotted spoon and set aside on a plate for 10 minutes.

- Increase the temperature of the oil to 180°C/350°F. Return the chips to the hot oil and fry for a further 3–4 minutes, or until golden and crispy. Remove from the oil with a slotted spoon and tip the chips on to a plate lined with kitchen paper to remove excess oil. Season with salt (or Salt and Pepper Seasoning, page 214) and serve.

FRENCH-FRIED ONION RINGS

Serves 1

250g self-raising flour
½ teaspoon sea salt
½ teaspoon MSG
Pinch of ground white pepper
225–275ml cold water
Oil for deep-frying
1 large onion, peeled and sliced into rings

- Put the self-raising flour, sea salt, MSG and white pepper in a large bowl, mix briefly, then gradually add the water, whisking well until a slightly thick batter is formed. Add more flour if the batter is too thin, or more water if the batter is too thick.

- Heat the oil for deep-frying to 170°C/340°F.

- Dip each onion ring in the batter until fully coated, drop carefully into the hot oil and fry for about 5 minutes or until crispy and golden.

- Remove from the oil using a slotted spoon, drain off any excess oil and arrange the onion rings on a plate lined with kitchen paper. Serve with Sweet and Sour Sauce (page 200).

STIR-FRIED BEANSPROUTS

Serves 1

1 large handful beansprouts (about 150g)
1 tablespoon vegetable oil
¼ large onion, thinly sliced
½ teaspoon sea salt
½ teaspoon MSG
1 teaspoon oyster sauce
½ teaspoon dark soy sauce
1 generous teaspoon chopped Garlic in Oil (page 211)
Pinch of ground white pepper
Pinch of ground black pepper
Pinch of Chinese 5-spice
1 spring onion, thinly sliced
2 teaspoons rice wine
Dash of sesame oil (optional)

- Put the beansprouts in a sieve and slowly pour 500ml boiling water over them. Drain and set aside.

- Heat a wok or large frying pan over a medium to high heat. Add the vegetable oil, then add the sliced onion and the drained beansprouts and stir-fry for 20–30 seconds. Add the salt, MSG, oyster sauce, dark soy sauce, chopped garlic in oil, white pepper, black pepper and Chinese 5-spice and stir-fry for 30–40 seconds.

- Add the spring onion and mix well. Add the rice wine and mix once more. Transfer the stir-fried beansprouts to a serving plate, finish with sesame oil (if using) and serve.

GARLIC MUSHROOMS

Serves 1

2 tablespoons oyster sauce
1 teaspoon light soy sauce
1 teaspoon dark soy sauce
Pinch of ground white pepper
¼ teaspoon caster sugar
1 tablespoon vegetable oil
10–12 button mushrooms (about 125g), quartered or
   halved (depending on size)
¼ teaspoon MSG
1 generous tablespoon chopped Garlic in Oil (page 211)
200ml Light Chicken Stock (page 218), vegetable stock or
   water
1 tablespoon potato starch mixed with 2 tablespoons cold
   water
1 tablespoon rice wine

- Put the oyster sauce, light soy sauce, dark soy sauce, white pepper and caster sugar in a bowl, mix well and set aside.

- Heat a wok or large frying pan over a medium to high heat. Add the vegetable oil, then add the mushrooms and stir-fry for 2 minutes.

- Add the MSG and chopped garlic in oil and mix well. Add the prepared sauce and mix well once more. Add the stock or water, bring to the boil and simmer for 2 minutes or until the sauce reduces slightly. Gradually add some of the starch-and-water mix, stirring well until the sauce reaches the desired consistency (you may not need all the mix). Add the rice wine, stir through and serve.

STIR-FRIED BROCCOLI

This is by far my favourite way to eat broccoli.

Serves 1

½ broccoli (about 150g), cut into small florets
1 tablespoon vegetable oil
Pinch of sea salt
Pinch of MSG
1 generous tablespoon chopped Garlic in Oil (page 211)
1 teaspoon potato starch mixed with 1 tablespoon cold
    water
2 teaspoons rice wine
Dash of Aromatic Oil (page 212) or sesame oil
1 teaspoon toasted white sesame seeds (optional)

Sauce

2 teaspoons oyster sauce
1 teaspoon light soy sauce
2 tablespoons cold water

- Put the sauce ingredients in a bowl, mix well and set aside.

- Bring a large saucepan of water to the boil. When the water
  is boiling, add the broccoli florets. Bring back to the boil
  and simmer for 2 minutes. Drain through a colander and
  set the broccoli aside.

- Heat a wok or large frying pan over a medium to high heat, add the vegetable oil and swirl it well around the pan. Add the broccoli florets and stir-fry for 30 seconds, then add the sea salt, MSG and chopped garlic in oil and mix well. Add the prepared sauce and stir-fry for 30 seconds. Gradually add the some of the starch-and-water mix, stirring well until the sauce reaches the desired consistency (you may not need all the mix). Add the rice wine and aromatic oil or sesame oil and mix well once more. Transfer the stir-fried broccoli to a serving plate, garnish with toasted sesame seeds (if using) and serve.

STIR-FRIED BAMBOO SHOOTS
AND WATER CHESTNUTS

This simple side dish is a quick and tasty way to add some vegetables to your fakeaway feast.

Serves 1

1 tablespoon vegetable oil
¼ large onion, roughly chopped
½ tin bamboo shoots, rinsed and drained (about 60g)
½ tin water chestnuts, rinsed and drained (about 60g)
Pinch of sea salt
Pinch of MSG
Pinch of white pepper
¼ teaspoon caster sugar
1 teaspoon potato starch mixed with 1 tablespoon cold
    water
1 teaspoon rice wine
Dash of Aromatic Oil (page 212) or sesame oil

Sauce
2 teaspoons oyster sauce
½ teaspoon light soy sauce
Dash of dark soy sauce
75ml cold water

- Put the sauce ingredients in a bowl, mix well and set aside.

- Heat a wok or large frying pan over a medium to high heat, add the vegetable oil and swirl it well around the pan. Add the chopped onion, bamboo shoots and water chestnuts and stir-fry for 30–40 seconds. Add the sea salt, MSG, white pepper and caster sugar and mix well.

- Add the prepared sauce, bring to the boil and simmer for 30–40 seconds. Gradually add the starch-and-water mix (you may not need all the mix). Add the rice wine and aromatic oil or sesame oil, mix well once more and serve.

PRAWN CRACKERS

You'll find large boxes of ready-to-cook prawn crackers in your local Chinese supermarket. The oil temperature needs to be very hot to fry these quickly, so I prefer to use a smaller pan and less oil and cook them 1 or 2 at a time. This takes a little longer but means less oil is wasted after cooking. You can, if desired, heat a larger pan of oil and fry many more crackers simultaneously.

Makes 20 prawn crackers

200ml vegetable oil
20 ready-to-cook prawn crackers

- Heat the oil in a pan to 195°C/385°F. Carefully drop 1 or 2 ready-to-cook prawn crackers in the pan and push them through the oil with a slotted spoon – they should puff up almost immediately and become large and crisp. Remove from the oil with a slotted spoon and set aside on a plate lined with kitchen paper to soak up excess oil. Repeat the process until all the prawn crackers are fried.

- Let the prawn crackers stand for 5 minutes, during which time they'll cool down and crisp up further. Serve immediately, or store in a sealed container at room temperature for up to 2 days.

SAUCES

With crispy chicken, wings, spare ribs, mini spring rolls, king prawns or just a bowl of chips or prawn crackers, a tasty sauce can turn something simple into an irresistible snack or meal. This chapter includes recipes for some classic sauces that you can combine with other recipes in the book to create your ultimate Chinese takeaway flavour combination.

SWEET AND SOUR SAUCE

This simple sweet and sour sauce takes just a few minutes to make and is coloured with beetroot to add natural colour and sweetness. You can tweak this sauce to suit your taste by making it sweeter with sugar or make it more sour with vinegar.

Makes 1 portion (about 225ml)

100ml water
50ml pineapple juice or syrup (from a tin)
3 tablespoons caster sugar
1 tablespoon dark brown sugar
20ml distilled clear malt vinegar
¼ teaspoon beetroot powder mixed with 1 tablespoon water
1 tablespoon potato starch mixed with 2 tablespoons cold water
1–2 pineapple pieces (from a tin)

- Put the water and pineapple juice or syrup in a saucepan and bring to the boil. When the mix is boiling, add the white and brown sugar and mix well. Reduce the heat to low and simmer for 3 minutes. Add the vinegar and mix well. Add the beetroot-powder-and-water mix and stir well once again.

- Increase the heat to medium-high and gradually add some of the starch-and-water mix, stirring through the simmering sauce until it reaches the desired consistency (you may not need all the mix). Add the pineapple pieces and pour the sweet and sour sauce into a serving bowl.

- Serve with Chicken Balls (page 30), Pork Balls (page 34), Prawn Toast (page 63), Large Pancake Rolls (page 50), Crispy Chicken Wings (page 52) or simply with Prawn Crackers (page 198).

- The sauce will keep well in the fridge for up to 2 days and can be reheated gently (you may need to add a little water when reheating if the sauce is thick). The sauce doesn't freeze well.

SWEET CHILLI DIPPING SAUCE

Makes about 200ml

2 tablespoons rice wine
2 tablespoons fish sauce
100ml rice wine vinegar
150g caster sugar
3 teaspoons dried chilli flakes
50ml water
1 tablespoon potato starch mixed with 2 tablespoons cold
   water

- Put the rice wine, fish sauce, rice wine vinegar, sugar, chilli flakes and water in a saucepan and mix well.

- Bring to the boil over a medium to high heat, then reduce the heat to medium-low and simmer for 8–10 minutes, or until the sauce is slightly reduced. Increase the heat to medium and gradually add the starch-and-water mix to the simmering sauce, stirring well until the sauce reaches the desired consistency (you may not need all the mix).

- Set the sauce aside to cool completely. The sweet chilli sauce will keep well in the fridge for up to 1 month.

SATAY SAUCE

Makes 1 portion (about 225ml)

1 tablespoon Chinese-style Curry Paste (page 215)
½ teaspoon caster sugar
½ teaspoon light soy sauce
½ teaspoon dark soy sauce
½ teaspoon oyster sauce
25g creamed coconut
200ml water
1 teaspoon chopped Garlic in Oil (page 211)
25g Jimmy's saté sauce
25g smooth or crunchy peanut butter
2 teaspoons rice wine

- Put the curry paste, sugar, light soy sauce, dark soy sauce, oyster sauce, creamed coconut and water in a saucepan. Bring to the boil over a medium heat, then reduce the heat to low and simmer for 1 minute.

- Add the chopped garlic in oil, saté sauce and peanut butter. Mix well until combined and simmer for 1 minute. Add the rice wine to finish and your satay sauce is ready to serve.

- The sauce will keep well in the fridge for up to 2 days, or in the freezer for up to 1 month. Reheat gently until piping hot, adding a little water during reheating if the sauce is too thick.

PEKING SAUCE

Makes 1 portion

2½ tablespoons tomato ketchup
2 tablespoons O.K. sauce
1 teaspoon hoisin sauce
1 tablespoon Worcestershire sauce
1 tablespoon golden syrup
1 teaspoon rice wine
2 teaspoons rice wine vinegar
¼ teaspoon smoked garlic powder
Pinch of MSG
¼ teaspoon beetroot powder
175ml pork stock (page 56) or water
1 tablespoon potato starch mixed with 2 tablespoons cold
    water

- Put the tomato ketchup, O.K. sauce, hoisin sauce, Worcestershire sauce, golden syrup, rice wine, rice wine vinegar, smoked garlic powder, MSG, beetroot powder and stock or water in a saucepan. Bring to the boil over a medium to high heat, then reduce the heat to low and simmer the sauce for 2 minutes.

- Increase the heat to medium-high and gradually add some of the starch-and-water mix, stirring it through the simmering sauce until the sauce reaches the desired thickness (you may not need all the mix). Pour the finished sauce over Fried Pork Spare Ribs (page 56) or serve with crispy chicken or king prawns.

- The sauce will keep well in the fridge for up to 2 days, or in the freezer for up to 1 month. Reheat gently until piping hot, adding a little water during reheating if the sauce is too thick.

CHINESE-STYLE BBQ SAUCE

Makes 1 portion

2 tablespoons hoisin sauce
2 tablespoons tomato ketchup
1 tablespoon golden syrup
2 tablespoons caster sugar
1 tablespoon soft dark brown sugar
150ml pork stock (page 56) or water
1 tablespoon oyster sauce
1/2 teaspoon light soy sauce
1/2 teaspoon dark soy sauce
1/4 teaspoon Chinese 5-spice
1/4 teaspoon ground white pepper
1/4 teaspoon MSG
1/4 teaspoon smoked garlic powder
1/2 teaspoon beetroot powder
Pinch of sea salt
1 teaspoon rice wine
1 tablespoon potato starch mixed with 2 tablespoons cold water

- Put the hoisin sauce, tomato ketchup, golden syrup, caster sugar, brown sugar, pork stock or water, oyster sauce, light soy sauce, dark soy sauce, Chinese 5-spice, white pepper, MSG, smoked garlic powder, beetroot powder, sea salt and rice wine in a saucepan, mix well over a medium to high heat until the mix begins to boil.

- Reduce the heat to medium and simmer the sauce for 2 minutes, stirring well until the sugars have dissolved. Gradually add some of the starch-and-water mix, stirring well to thicken until the sauce reaches the desired consistency (you may not need all the mix).

- Pour the BBQ sauce generously over Fried Pork Spare Ribs (page 56) or Crispy Chicken Wings (page 52).

- The sauce will keep well in the fridge for up to 2 days, or I the freezer for up to 1 month. Reheat gently until piping hot, adding a little water during reheating if the sauce is too thick.

CHINESE-STYLE CURRY SAUCE

Makes 1 portion

50g Chinese-style Curry Paste (page 215)
225ml Light Chicken Stock (page 218)
¼ teaspoon sea salt
¼ teaspoon MSG
¼ teaspoon caster sugar

- Put the Chinese curry paste, light chicken stock, sea salt, MSG and sugar in a saucepan and heat over a low to medium heat, whisking constantly, until the curry paste dissolves and the sauce thickens slightly and is piping hot. Add a little more water if the sauce becomes too thick, or cook it for longer or add more curry paste if it becomes too thin. For a smoother sauce, pass it through a fine sieve before serving (optional).

- The sauce will keep well in the fridge for up to 2 days, or in the freezer for up to 1 month. Reheat gently until piping hot, adding a little water during reheating if the sauce is too thick.

OILS, PASTES
AND EXTRAS

TOASTED CASHEW NUTS

1 handful raw cashew nuts (about 30g)

- Heat a dry wok or large frying pan over a medium heat. Add the raw cashew nuts and toast in the dry pan for 2–3 minutes, stirring often until aromatic and nicely coloured. Tip the toasted cashew nuts onto a small plate and set aside. Use for Kung Po (page 127) or add to your favourite stir-fry dishes.

- Alternatively, the raw cashew nuts can be fried in hot oil (180°C/350°F) for 1–2 minutes until golden. Remove from the oil with a slotted spoon, drain off any excess oil on kitchen paper and set aside for use as above.

GARLIC IN OIL

This garlic oil is useful in two ways – the oil can be added to marinades or used to finish chow mein or fried rice dishes, while the chopped garlic itself can be added to stir-fries and salt and chilli dishes. Look for larger packs of dried chopped garlic in Chinese supermarkets which are both superior to and less expensive than traditional supermarket brands.

Makes about 450g

100g dried chopped garlic
400ml water
250ml vegetable oil
Pinch of sea salt

- Put the dried chopped garlic in a large heatproof bowl. Boil the water, pour it over the chopped garlic, mix well and set aside for 5 minutes. Strain the garlic through a fine sieve.

- Put the garlic in a saucepan and cover with the vegetable oil. Place over a medium heat and let the mixture come to a sizzle, then reduce the heat to low and slowly fry the garlic for 10–12 minutes, until aromatic. Add the salt and mix through. Set aside to cool completely, pour into a food-safe container with a tight-fitting lid and store in the fridge for up to 1 month.

AROMATIC OIL

This seasoned oil can be used as an alternative to sesame oil to finish chow mein, fried rice or salt and chilli dishes, as desired.

Indian bay leaf (tej patta) is a pungent leaf which has a very different aromatic profile from European bay leaves, adding a sweet aniseed and cinnamon flavour to the oil.

Makes 250ml oil

250ml vegetable oil
1 small onion, roughly chopped
6 garlic cloves, roughly chopped
1 small piece of fresh ginger, roughly chopped (about the equivalent size of 3 garlic cloves)
1 spring onion, halved
¼ cinnamon stick
2 whole star anise
1 Indian bay leaf (tej patta)

- Put the vegetable oil, chopped onion, garlic, ginger, spring onion, cinnamon, star anise and Indian bay leaf in a saucepan. Place over a medium to high heat and heat until the ingredients begin to sizzle in the pan. Reduce the heat to low and simmer for 20–30 minutes, or until the onions are well browned. Strain the oil through a fine sieve and set the oil aside to cool completely. The oil will keep well in a sealed container in the fridge for up to 1 month.

CHILLI OIL

This deeply coloured spiced oil can be added to any stir-fry, soup or noodle dish to good effect.

Makes 75ml chilli oil

¼ teaspoon ground Szechuan pepper
1 teaspoon dried chilli flakes
¼ teaspoon smoked paprika powder
¼ teaspoon smoked garlic powder
1 teaspoon mild chilli powder
¼ teaspoon Chinese 5-spice
¼ teaspoon sea salt
¼ teaspoon MSG
75ml vegetable oil

- Put the ground Szechuan pepper, dried chilli flakes, paprika, smoked garlic powder, mild chilli powder, Chinese 5-spice, sea salt and MSG in a heatproof bowl, mix briefly and set aside.

- Heat the vegetable oil in a small saucepan to about 120°C/250°F. Carefully pour the hot oil over the prepared spices (the spices will foam a little in the bowl). Mix well, then set aside to cool. Cover and store in the fridge for up to 2 weeks.

SALT AND PEPPER SEASONING

This aromatic seasoning is essential for 'salt and chilli' dishes.

Makes about 180g

6 tablespoons sea salt
1 whole star anise
2 tablespoons MSG
3 tablespoons caster sugar
1½ teaspoons ground white pepper
1½ tablespoons Chinese 5-spice
1½ teaspoons Chinese ginger powder
¼ teaspoon extra-hot chilli powder
1 teaspoon smoked garlic powder

- Heat a seasoned carbon-steel wok or large frying pan over a medium to high heat. Add the sea salt and whole star anise and stir-fry for about 10 minutes, until the salt changes colour and the star anise aroma is noticeable. Pour the toasted salt into a large heatproof bowl and set aside to cool completely (be careful, the toasted salt will be HOT!).

- Once the toasted salt is completely cooled, add the MSG, sugar, white pepper, Chinese 5-spice, Chinese ginger powder, extra-hot chilli powder and smoked garlic powder. Mix thoroughly and transfer to a food-safe container. Seal with a lid. The salt and pepper seasoning mix will keep well in a cool, dark cupboard for up to 3 months.

CHINESE-STYLE CURRY PASTE

Makes about 900g

400ml sunflower oil
1 onion, sliced
1 carrot, sliced
1 celery stalk, sliced
2 whole star anise
¼ cinnamon stick
1 Indian bay leaf (tej patta)
4 garlic cloves, sliced
3 tablespoons tinned fruit cocktail
1½ teaspoons mild chilli powder
1 teaspoon ground turmeric
¼ teaspoon smoked garlic powder
¼ teaspoon Chinese 5-spice
1 teaspoon sea salt
¼ teaspoon MSG
2 teaspoons caster sugar
50g creamed coconut
120g curry powder (I like the brand Eastern Star)
300g plain flour

- Put the sunflower oil, onion, carrot, celery, star anise, cinnamon stick and Indian bay leaf in a large saucepan. Place over a medium to high heat just until the ingredients begin to sizzle, then immediately turn the heat down to the lowest possible setting. Fry for 10 minutes. Add the sliced garlic and fry for another 20 minutes.

- Remove the star anise, cinnamon stick and bay leaf from the pan with a slotted spoon. Add the fruit cocktail, chilli powder, turmeric, smoked garlic powder, Chinese 5-spice, sea salt, MSG and sugar. Mix well, then remove from the heat and use a stick blender to blend the mixture until smooth.

- Add the creamed coconut and stir well until fully melted. Add the curry powder and mix well until the spices are fully incorporated, allowing the spices to cook for 30–40 seconds.

- Gradually begin to add the plain flour, a third at a time. Mix well, incorporating the flour fully into the mix. The curry paste will start to become thick and dry and will take some effort to stir. At this stage the spices and flour must be cooked out fully – cook the mixture over a low heat for 30–40 minutes, stirring and mashing the curry paste often. As the spices and flour begin to cook out, you'll see the spiced oil separating from the paste slightly and the aroma will become fragrant. Don't skip this step! Give your curry paste love and attention during this time.

- Once the curry paste is cooked and cooled, it will keep well in the fridge for up to 2 weeks, but it is best stored in the freezer, where it will keep well for up to 3 months. The mix will stay loose enough when frozen that portions can be scooped out with a spoon if the paste is frozen in one container, though you can freeze it in 50g portions if you wish.

• Use to make Chinese-style Curry Sauce (page 146) or a main-meal curry dish.

LIGHT CHICKEN STOCK

Makes about 2 litres

Throughout this book you'll find many recipes which call for light chicken stock. You can make your own by following this recipe, or use any good-quality shop-bought unsalted or low-salt chicken stock. If the stock you have is salty, dilute it with an equal amount of water, or adjust salt levels in your chosen recipe to suit.

> 4 bone-in chicken thighs (500–600g) (leave the skin on for a richer stock, or remove for a thinner lighter stock)
> ½ small onion, sliced
> 2 spring onions, cut in half
> 1 garlic clove, crushed
> 1 small piece of ginger (around the same size as a garlic clove)
> 2.5 litres water
> ½ teaspoon sea salt

- Put the chicken thighs, sliced onion, spring onions, garlic and ginger in a large saucepan. Cover with the 2.5 litres water, bring to the boil, reduce the heat to low and simmer the stock for 3 hours, spooning off any foam that forms on the surface occasionally during cooking.

- Strain the stock to remove the chicken and vegetables, then add the salt to the strained stock and mix well. Set aside to cool completely, then portion as desired and refrigerate or freeze. The stock will keep well in the fridge for up to 3 days or in the freezer for up to 3 months.

• Soups and stir-fry dishes in this book typically call for 200–300ml of light chicken stock or thereabouts, so you may choose to freeze the stock in portions of this size.

BANANA OR PINEAPPLE FRITTER

Serves 1

125g self-raising flour
100–150ml cold water
Oil for deep-frying
1 banana, cut lengthways into three pieces, or 2 tinned
    pineapple rings
2 tablespoons golden syrup

- Put the self-raising flour in a large bowl. Gradually add the water, whisking well until a thick batter is formed. Add more water if the batter is too thick, or more flour if the batter is too thin.

- Heat the oil for deep-frying to 170°C/340°F. Dip each banana piece or pineapple piece in the batter until fully coated, drop carefully into the hot oil and fry for about 5 minutes or until crispy and golden.

- Remove from the oil using a slotted spoon and put the battered banana or pineapple pieces in a large bowl. Add the golden syrup and toss gently to coat before serving.

GROW YOUR OWN BEANSPROUTS

With very little effort you can grow beansprouts in just a few days! They won't reach the size of some of the beansprouts you might find in your local supermarket, but they'll be just as tasty and far fresher!

Simple sprouting trays can be purchased from garden stores or online, as well as organic mung beans, which you can use for sprouting. Wash a large handful of mung beans in water two or three times, drain and add to a sprouting tray. Put the tray in a dark place and pour fresh water through the sprouts daily for 3–5 days as they grow.

Rinse the sprouts well before adding them to your favourite stir-fry or chow mein dishes.

ACKNOWLEDGEMENTS

When my first book was published in 2010, I wouldn't have dared to dream that I'd still be getting to do this more than ten years later. Thanks to the encouragement and support I've had from readers, my obsession with cooking and recreating dishes has grown every day. I hope I've gained more knowledge and experience over that time also, and can share some of those new ideas and cooking tips with you in this book.

When it comes to Chinese takeaway-style cooking, praise and gratitude has to go to the former owners of The Eastern Legend in Glasgow, my takeaway of choice in my younger years, as well as Andy Cheung, chef and owner of Wok Star in Glasgow's south side. When it comes to delivering tasty dishes that inspire, Andy is right up there with the very best of them, and if you ever find yourself in Glasgow, I'd highly recommend a visit.

As always, my fiancée Rebecca deserves huge thanks for putting up with my food obsessions and never-ending questions, as do my other close family and friends who are always enthusiastic when I have food pictures or conversation to share: Margaret, Frank, Stephen, Deborah, Mike, Roisin, Christy, Audrey, John, Sam, Larraine, Phoebe, Adele, Iain, Frank and Alison Mooney, Ian and Alexx, Kirsty Bowker, Lisa, Lou, and Louise Boyle.

Thanks also to you, for reading this book! If you try any of the recipes, I hope you'll be glad to have done so.

INDEX